Poetically Correct:
Banned by The Free Press

By: Ciera S. Louise

Order this book online at www.trafford.com
or email orders@trafford.com

Most Trafford titles are also available at major online book retailers.

Printed in the United States of America.

ISBN: 978-1-4269-7389-5 (sc)
ISBN: 978-1-4269-7390-1 (e)

Trafford rev. 01/29/2015

www.trafford.com

North America & international
toll-free: 1 888 232 4444 (USA & Canada)
fax: 812 355 4082

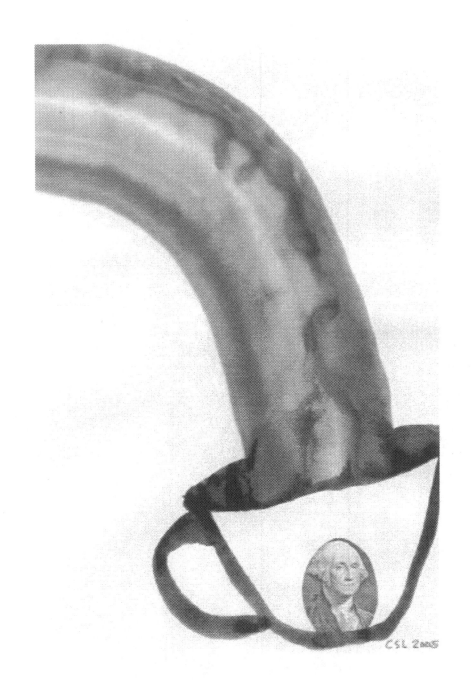

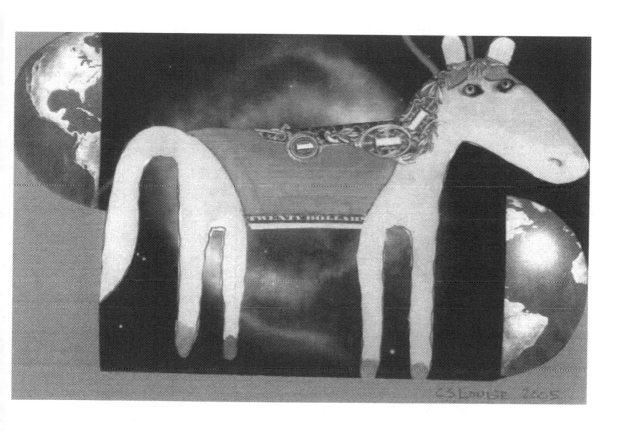

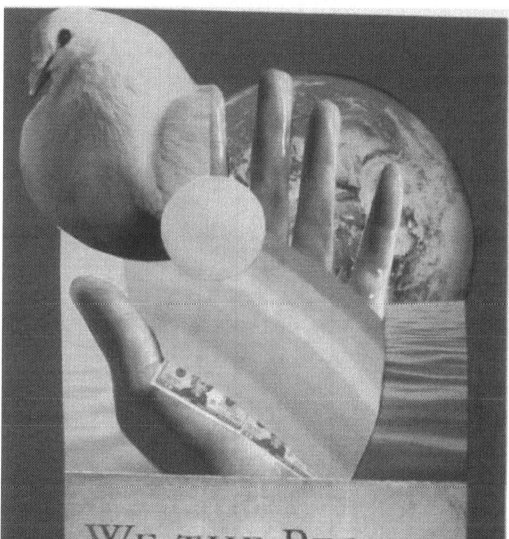

TABLE OF CONTENTS

BOOK INTRODUCTION

This is a continuation of poetry in the chronological order of my life since I was age 14 in 1977. I continue to observe, discover and question why things, particularly people, are the way they are. Evil senseless acts of cruelty and violence are always perplexing to me. The crimes against animals completely astound me. I don't cry and whine like I used to. There's no point in arguing with the Omnipotent One, whatever you think that Persona or Energy to be. Poetry is my way of sorting things out. I have written for and about people primarily. If there is an incident in my life, I write it out in this way. It has been an unusual life fraught with much injustice up until I passed my fortieth year. I am much happier than ever in my life. I'm still poor, disabled, and growing old, but there is much more joy to be found and therefore I focus on these wonderful things, many of which money cannot buy. We are blessed with so much that we could never give back nearly as much to our fellow human beings, animals and planet earth. Sadly, many people harm all of those things. However, there are those shining gems amongst us, imperfectly beautiful. They exude a loving disposition in spite of what they own, who they know, or what they look like. Some of them do have money beyond necessity and many do not. Giving is kind, expecting nothing in return is kinder. Anonymous giving is the kindest of all. It brings hope and faith in humanity to those who wondered if there existed any such hope. I love those of you like this. I haven't come to love my enemy, I daresay, but I have learned a strange compassion for their suffering and ultimate unrest. I wish no harm and do no harm if I can avoid it.

Ciera S. Louise

May 17, 2011

We Shall Overcome

I sit in the emergency room
My daughter sleeps again
They can't see her suffering
So we'll have to sit 'til when
Into this eternity
Where no one seems to care
The sadness makes me tired
I drift away from here
To a place that is serene
Where urgency is gone
I'm just an older mother
No longer quite so strong
She doesn't know I'd die for her
Or that I'm afraid of those
Who distort my every move
This evil they impose
To separate our souls within
Rip my heart asunder
How my friends can't understand
Or hear the angels' thunder
I'm calling in the wilderness
Can you see me for the crowd?
I'm the self-conscious wanderer
Chanting prayers out loud
I plead out to the Universe
To circle 'round us here
Send me Ariel of old
Please take away this fear
And if they do destroy me
My body is no more
Guide my child to the Light
Show her the ancient door
On the other side she's safe
Skyla Dove above the earth
No shadows shall forsake her
Or lie about her birth
My spirit shall stand by her
And slay the Devil low
I am empowered now
More than they'll ever know.

Holy Days To Silent Nights

Devil out on Washington St.
Lived to see others perish
It's so close to Christmas
I wonder what we'll cherish
Will it be the gifts or lights
That brings us all together?
Or will phantoms of misfortune
Bring gray and icy weather?
To mock the season held so dear
While I mourn the withering pine
Never quite ready to exchange
My gifts for bloody wine
You have your little secrets
All year tell little lies
Now 'tis time to celebrate
For your manger baby cries
Either way you follow yonder
There's a sermon on every hill
Hypocrites so full of deceit
Know nothing of good will
I have no reason for this rhyme
But for front page news again
That reminds us of our tendency
To hostility now and then
A bulb goes out and all shall too
An ornament lay shattered
Garland wrapped so greedily
That none of it has mattered
Sit in this holy moment
With silent revelations
Leads you to a graveyard
To face the constellations
From where we all return
When all is said and done
Sleep in heavenly peace
When all become as One.

You Who Subvert

Be brief and diplomatic
Smile though it's unfair
But I didn't paint my nails
And tidy up my hair
Don't really want this job
My ass is what's for hire
All those savings liquidate
The moment I retire
Give me a barter system
Community made strong
Where everyone is abled
And the elderly belong
Some say it Communism
When you deface our money
But when a weak man says this
It's both sad and rather funny
Grandma does wear combat boots
And I won't wear a bra
Nylons and spiked heels
Will get you just so far
Stick figures are an easy draw
This bait is unappealing
Think of all the compromise
Gift of life that you're concealing
Like a veil and tightened shroud
You're bound up in the tomb
Because for those like you
The planet has less room
To breathe and simply speak
Dance for all you are worth
You're employed to be benevolent
And protect the blessed earth
Never think they own you
Do no more and never less
'Cause the Reaper always wins
For guilt will know no rest
I'm not so pessimistic
When Karma runs its course
And every politician
Has a fate I shall endorse.

Someone Cut The Line

I hold onto the phone
Though no one is there
What do I have to do
To get away from here?
Pack a few boxes
Leave each vital note
Give up on the dream
They'll care what I wrote
Take good care of my Love
I'm leaving this plane
Won't need a suitcase
Not even a name
Just another piece of waste
That stumbled and fell
If you ever really knew me
You know it's just as well
I stop fighting Destiny
Gasping for thick air
Disillusioned to think
This would ever be fair
Lying on the floor
I imagine I'm gone
Imagine it's just right
I'm finally not wrong
Winter has buried me
Under snow and dusty ice
I'm that dirty snowbank
Ignored in this life

Of traffic and hum
Chaos all around
Like a dead standing tree
I make not a sound
Merely go on to witness
The life I once had
That I never truly lived
Feeling ever so sad
Angel hear me now
You see within my soul
Envelop me in serenity
Take me and make me whole
No more pain or suffering
Carry my broken shell
I have failed this journey
Lift me from this hell.

Shine Your Light On Me

Loving wisdom of an aged companion
Be it either or both in body and soul
Is to have life's greatest gift of All
That takes us to Death happy and whole
Numbered days marked their course
And a broken-stemmed rose did bow
Beautifully frozen in a moment of Grace
I sing unwritten Psalms of Now
Every breath has been so labored
Presdestined for the Lover's Shrine
I claim not and take not these things
Nor your linen which is not mine
This body has been a temple of doom
But still all my dreams took wing
For Time is swept up in the Shadows
As all Beings crave the Spring
O' New England winter is callous!
Paralyzing Our naked youth
As we have been so condemned
Prisoners can't confess the Truth
To pass through fire then ice
We weather all the storms
Being human I've paid the price
I've filled out all the forms
For the seeking of absolute freedom
Believe there's another side

To every frost-bitten face
Lined rows of broken tides
Let Us stand against the wind
We are the noble martyrs of pain
We are heroes when we awaken
Baptized in promised rain
If you wonder what you have done
To deserve the season's beating
It's for what you do not do
Self-indulgence is self-defeating
Give your coat to the broken man
Mother him in such Divine
Intoxicate his fantasy
With rainbows in his wine
For as we die we are reborn
The majestic trees do testify
You love me and I love you
Our love shall lift Us high.

Living Karma

I love You
You love Me
When you go to Them
They twist your words
As evil intent
As spikes to my heart
They are not your friends
Or confidantes
Nor be mine
Do not betray my Love
Lest you betray yourself
They will have you dig your grave
Before you'll ever dine with Them
Even so
Their food will cause you to regurgitate
For all that is untrue
Cannot survive
Be Love and Truth
Know Peace and Harmony
I am always with You
For you,
    beside you,
Never against your tides
I will block the shadow
Pulling at your feet
To devour you
In Death while you are alive
Standing, sitting, or lying
O' Guardian Angel
Of unseen doors Eternal
Shine as the Sun
Be One
As I have forgiven
Tho' mute in my forgiveness
I have never
Will never
Forsake your Light
Your beauty
Your strength
For earthly gain
For You are all that matters.

Clipped Wings Cannot Fly

Women! It is not beautiful
Rather sorrowful to acquiesce
To the Powers that oppress you!
To sweat for the Masters of Corruption
Get off your running wheel
Like the rodent who discovers
She remains in an aquarium of glass
To see, but not touch
To know, but have no voice
To cry, and not be heard
    The Sun sets on the West
    On graves of your ancestors
    Who fought for Lady Liberty
    Now taken from you
    By the Politician
    Who allies with the Churches of Oppression
    Stifling you into submission
Hold your children close
Or they will be slaughtered
In unGodly ways
    Lift the sparrow in your palm
    Your kiss brings him life
    Your Love sets him back on wing
    Do not forsake your true beauty
    For the dictates of money, war, or greed
    That continue to rip Us apart
    With nowhere to run for shelter
Women! Claim your position upright
Forthright
Birthright
Angels of Mother Earth
Beautiful be not weak
To surrender your power
    Nurse Us back to Unity
    Neighbor loving neighbor
    Rich loving poor
    Parent loving child
    Loving Thyself as you are
    Before God
    Naked and glorified
    Unfettered as a flower
    Testifying the I Am
O' men!

Vengeance Is Mind Says The Lord

Friends are earned, more valuable than money
If The Government weren't so cruel, they'd be rather funny
They say you'll get retirement, only if you're one of the few
Who don't incur medical expense after age sixty-two
So you think the poor get mercy and are given free aid?
Truth is it's impossible to access or win their charade!
They condemn the mafia for the loan shark and racketeer
But credit card companies are immune with no fear
They sell you alcohol, the deadliest of drugs
And lock up sad pot users as if they were thugs
How about the medical care not afforded to all?
Or homeless families put on hold when they call?
Pleading to guide them out of the poverty way
But given paperwork games where rules change each day
I've seen our old people, blind with trembling hands
Single mothers condemned, mentally ill no one understands
These are our neighbors shivering in the cold
With minimal fuel assistance and ragged blankets to hold
Instead of a helping hand lifting their spirit up
They're given outdated food like vinegar in their cup
There is no true charity where nonprofit is gain
Being criminal is insinuated when you're asked to explain
Why you hold your head high and won't bow to the few
Sheiks of America controlling mass media too
I will love my brother no matter the price
Politicians rot in their graves, their treasure is blight
And in the eye of God their soul will be made known
For destroying the planet their bread shall be stone
So next time you're bombed, remember money can't replace
Love you have lost in wars of disgrace
Cherish your children, future casualties of the Lie
For you've been totally led like fat sheep that will die
It is time to rise up, unite and not divide
You hold the real power of the American pride
And though we're not perfect our goal is The Constitution
Ultimately there will come the Christ Revolution
The Beast is up front and rules over you
Open your eyes and fear not what is true
Unplug the cable that keeps him so strong
Family is more precious and where you belong.

Joan Of Arc

Burned once
Lived twice
My temple knows the price
To stand among men
A warrior again
Calling out you heard
Above the mockingbird
A message of peace
Mother Earth you release!
Aphrodite rise
Above ancient lies
Wrap 'round our child
For Mona Lisa smiled
Truth be made known
The man stands alone
No longer we fear
Revelation is near
Roman Empire had fell
To the tolling bell
Chain link an arm
I'll keep you from harm
If you simply listen
To the feminine mission
Not as rebel or enemy told
Not for power, money or gold
But peace like a river
Undamned to deliver
God and Goddess Supreme
You must wake from your dream
The fortress keeps you in
Keeps you down for The Sin
Lie be made known
On a tablet of stone
The etching and wretching
Of blood and bone
Hung once
Stabbed twice
Like the image of Christ
Be thee on my left
Be thee on my right
Be thee of wisdom
For Thine is the Light.

In Memory Of Irving:
Inside A Guinea Pig

Blessed be the Soul
Of One so tender
Tears of Love
As we remember
A part of us
We breathed you in
Felt your warmth
Against our skin
A smell so sweet
As a child to mother
A fluttering heartbeat
Precious life like no other
We carry you inside
Eternal part of our soul
We thank you Dear Irving
For making us whole
Now the angels have come
We shall honor your flight
Out of this bondage
And into the Light
God lifts You high
His plan so Divine
Small seed of pure Love
Be forever mine.

Above All Be Low

Give me one black crow and any white moth
I'll fast for three days then feed me broth
I'll rub your feet and encircle you in Light
Set you on the path that cuts the night
And when they stare yet understand naught
Remember sacred mantras you've been taught
You are untouchable as the radiant witness
To above and below, immune to sickness
Nowhere is home, everywhere strife
You among the dead were brought to life
The We and Us are your distant kin
Close in spirit though sculpted by sin
You are admonished for losing your name
Written on lit walls of the eternal flame
And if they hate you because of me
They resent the Wisdom that sets you free
While they in bondage hiss and moan
Spiral downward, clawing stone
Feel such sadness, for they are lost
Sold their soul at any cost
They shall return as human, plant or beast
Until self-pride has been released
For now I shall love the moth and crow
The Dog
The Rats
And all below.

Abberon Lost

Ab'ron
Ab'ron
Why do you call?
I see not the message
On this vacant wall
I walk to and fro'
Look into every crack
Lean into it
Then turn back
Such a simple rhyme
Yet complex thought
I can't keep returning
To this empty spot
I've always discerned
In the universal breeze
The distant thunder
And whispering leaves
A confirmation spoken loud
Musical muse within the crowd
It's been many months
You've stricken me dumb
Catatonic and blind
Crippled and numb
Is it merely distraction
Of evil envy and wrath
That I should pause
On this righteous path?
Well dear Ab'ron
I must proceed
It's time to stop starting
To follow your lead
Return to me
If it be God's will
Otherwise I command you
To be still!

Division of Inhuman Services

If any person dislikes or envies you
There will be no debate
When you become the victim
For their phone call to the State
No matter your innocence
A "public servant" comes to scrutinize
For forty-five through sixty-days
You are on trial for these lies
This so-called "servant" must justify
Government funding these ways
Invading your privacy
Like some criminal for days
Even when you are finally cleared
Your unknown Accuser goes free!
Even though we have a law
That states this should not be (RSA 641:3)
Malicious reports are quite common
And have gotten out of control
Because no one gets punished
Except the targeted soul
Tell me about true justice
When they come to YOUR door
Because I can make a phone call
Like an anonymous whore
I too could be vindictive—this is okay
The State I live in says:
I can screw you for days!
I can even make a false claim!
Say I did it only with good intent
Now I'm free from prosecution! (RSA 161-F:47)
And you can get bent!
Yea to the divorcee and the jealous!
I'm told this is often the case
How about these liars
At least reimbursing the State?
Costing the working taxpayer
Once again wasted spending
Stop blaming welfare recipients
Look at the embezzlers you're defending
Because you are misled
Thieves ARE agents OF your System
Either reform or overthrow
Stand up and resist them!
Or YOU'LL find one day
ALL of YOUR rights are gone
BEWARE THEY ARE LYING!
And YOU are their pawn.

Camouflage In My Closet

How high can a bird fly?
How far can a dog run?
How long can a human
Stare into the Sun?
Or chase it to the rise
Of another abominable day
Where mankind is not worthy
To bequest his Soul pray
For another tomorrow of
Broken dreams and hypocrites
Dragging our nation
Down into the pits
Of devastation and war
History repeating itself
Where so many have so less
Freedom's determined by wealth
Woe to the Monarchy!
Liars they reign!
Our soldiers of misfortune
Our children dying in vain
I find myself pondering
Why a rose withers so soon
And people can't disappear
Or live on the moon
If I didn't distract to these
I'd spin like a tornado of rage
And you wouldn't be here
Turning this page.

Election Day 2004

Feel such sadness
For the flock
Our Shepherd be
A deadly hawk
Eagle and Dove
Abandon Us
Price the water
Serve Us dust
The land lay bare
No trees or grass
No shelter from
The killing blast
O' say how can you see?
Your lids are sewn shut!
The rockets' red glare
Represents what?
A snow-white banner
Spattered with blood
A little boy
Covered in mud
O' Death be not proud!
A proverbial condition
A psalmic moment
Self-inflicted decision
Ah! So hard to examine
One cannot inflect
Ego-Centers by Law
Must always project!
The coldest winter
I expect shall be
And spring beholds
No victory.

The Good News

Divisive reporting buzzards
I shall not lend my voice!
A place there is no peace
No space to make a choice
They're slanted and repulsive
So biased thus omitting
All of what is Truth
O' the crime they are committing!
You've come to fear your neighbor
You give charity to the thief
You purchase from Goliath
Yet it gives you no relief
'Cause he is standing strong
With a smelly green-glory smile
The poet says to simplify
With your brother reconcile
Give the gift of time
Tho' you think you have it not
Not all the news is grim
And Christmas can't be bought
Smile, hug and hold the door
Thank you please again
Children wipe your eyes
Let the holi-days begin
May their front page spark my fire
So I am warm and see the Light
While their lies go up in smoke
Like black angels of the Night
Peace on earth we pray
As evil sentinels do depart
The reason for all seasons
Is printed in my heart.

New Year, Old Soul

Make a new commitment
To celebrate your Friend
To integrate philosophy
A gentle hand extend
To those who are in need
Tho' you know not their name
Some are dressed too proper
Others seem so lame
No man is an island
The beginning was the Word
The Poet has been crucified
And yet you never heard
He stood upon a hill
His voice could calm the sea
Make every being still
Love all humanity
Your Enemy is exposed
A gossip and a liar
One who preaches war
Creates destructive fire
Be the body temporal
Angels are aware
The millennium has come
Redemption conquers fear
O' can you hear the nations
The Universal tongue?
Lend your song for Peace
Then may your will be done
In all of this extreme
I'm filled with gratitude
For the writers in our town
Who don't attend to feud
Unsung heroes behind the scenes
Doing what must be done
To counteract the terrorism
Bestowed on everyone
Our Father who Art in Heaven
Protect them in this storm
I am truly inadequate
As one in fleshly form
My pen is running dry
My hand does tremor so
God grant me the wisdom
That comes with letting go.

I Am Not An Angel

I am not an angel
Unintentional in verse
I never took the vow
For better or for worse
I am not an angel
Your gun should not be drawn
When did I offend you?
What did I do wrong?
O' yes, the one mistake
Was complaining the condition
But I am reinventing
The purpose of my mission
I am not an angel
Whether you love me
Or love me not
I am only human
Conformity my lot
Well, I'm slow to listen
To your Master of derision
I turn my back on him
Pledge allegiance with omission
I am not an angel
Tho' one comforts my aching heart
Led so to temptation
Separate from Thou Art
My Father does forgive me
For the fool I have been
I acknowledge my earthen plight
So I may fly again
Forty years I had to wait
The Enemy stood strong
Knocking at my door
Stifling my song
Angel not am I
But I can hear them sing
Poetry in harmony
Revealing everything
Above, below, beyond
Whispered to a scream
Within and without
In reality the dream.

A Trio It Be

Ratava was an avatar
Dog is Love you see?
Starting lines are here
This be your Destiny
Knowledge is not power
Strength is never strong
Can't elect what is ordained
The rights can be so wrong
Privacy is for invasion
Speech is far from free
Money is the luminary
The false Serenity
Bloodlines remain tainted
Transfusion leads to Death
Every man is gasping
For selling out his Breath
Oh whiddle down my riddle
Tweedle-Dee and Tweedle-Dumb
You know the late white rabbit
Was really Every One?
Yet who cares about the date
When all is said and done
When everything is meaningless
Not new under the sun?
The Gift shall stay unopened
Til you reason out the rhyme
Repetition is your master
The same mistake your crime
Listen to the silence
Be blind so you can see
The Kingdom in your midst
Be the circled Trinity.

Sentenced To Life

Tossing photographs
Across the floor
A suicide king
His crazy whore
Looking back
Nothing changed much
So in poverty and ruin
We remain untouched
It's twelve a.m.
My daughter cries
I fill her belly
And dry her eyes
My song is muted
By this intense pain
For tomorrow
We must pose again.

An Old Woman In New England

The fractured vase now stands alone
Once held the roses of this home
Withered bouquet pastel and dry
Painful memories that never die
For beauty sweet is but a day
To gaze upon then look away
Ashamed to age then bend and fall
Be less considered if seen at all
Useless wisdom this lore of Fate
Befalls each person poor or great
Counted out while counting down
Trapped within an aging frown
Old Man Winter has no heart
He lives to tear dim hopes apart
Broken pieces upon the floor
Please don't glue me anymore
I shan't hold water anyway
Please this time sweep me away.

Sunday Hypocrite

Father Winterling dresses in black
A casket figure who can't relax
With agonized face he preaches hope
Holds up the chalice like a telescope
But he can't see God this far below
Cursing February as he mumbles low
A congregation to stay intact
Must hear the truthful damning fact
Wind does injure and cold contagious
The cost of warmth behooves outrageous
Tell us a proverb while psalms we sing
Then solemnly swear at everything
The biased news a computerized game
Violent cartoons about a Dick and Jane
Out damn Spot! 'twas a Grimm Fairytale
Brainwashed believers out on bail
Bow to your landlord, boss and teacher
Your leader, pope and prison preacher
So sound it crazy this subliminal thrill?
At least I don't sell lies to bend your will
Curse the food-drugs-and latest tend
The expensive clothes of make-pretend
He's better than you best dressed oppressed
For then on Sunday be forgiven and blessed
Oh priestly statue so rigid and dead
My body and soul are not your bread
My blood not wine that you'll drink dry
Your unseen God has heard my cry.

Some Children Never Change

Bully
Antagonist, a
Sadistic
Troublemaker, so
Arrogant and
Repulsive, most
Deviant
    Take him off the bus!

Belligerent
Imp, a
Tease and
Cunning
Hussy
    Take her to the sty!

Attuned
Never
Insensitive to
Man unkind.
Appreciative
Loyal and
Simple
    Take them for example:

    Who's the real beast?

Oppressive Press

The Buyer and the Guardian
Climbed in bed together
Talked over how to misinform
The public for the better
Edit, chop or delete
Any writer that we hate
Particularly dumb poets
Who don't think we're so great
Backstab gossip and classified
We can't leave out the dead
Or the lottery for idiots
Whose taxes must be bled
Don't harm the rich or royal name!
But *do* slander the poor
A kind of evil that divides a home
We'll deliver door to door
So keep printing all your bias
Sleep deep in your made bed
You both deserve each other
For the tumors that you spread
Money is all you'll ever love!
You're Satan's printed best
The first to say that Jesus loves you
When you're all that He'd detest
Oh sweet reasoning rhyme
Our nation was built on you
Democracy *not* dictatorship
Shall see The People through!

Another Monarchy 2005

So the media can't get a true profile of the King?
When they're poised and aimed at everything?
He's killing *your* children while telling the Nations
This is what's 'Right' for public relations
He has murdered civilians in countries abroad
And justified it in his service to God
There's nothing Patriotic about this Act
Of absolute power and criminal tact
When we got bombed like sitting ducks
It should have been those political schmucks
A true Citizen won't accept this for long
Read your Constitution if you think I am wrong
It's being dismantled right under your nose
Jefferson warned the Monarchy grows
When checks and balances have been deleted
Your Democracy has been defeated
You must unite before it's too late
There's no class division when it comes to fate
There's US and Them—the symbolic red bear
He with wisdom and courage must have no fear.

Rhapsody Of Addiction

My cigarette was like a tortoise
Who should have been named Rigor Mortis
Slowly plodding for lack of breath
To the finish line perceived as Death
It wasn't until I got angry enough
That I could live without another puff
Of deceptive desire born of fire
Sold by the Empirical Lord of Liars
I still smell the residue of destruction
The stains and stares of this seduction
I was paying Them to kill Me as was designed!
How can something so small control my mind?
So next time you purchase this kind of relief
Know that a pizza or prescription can be just as brief
A pleasure and cure for all that stress
So you'll be fatter and less depressed!
This is the kind of thing I write
While Reality TV is on at night
Okay, it's not really ALL bad news
Cause you always have the power to refuse
To be bombarded in all the static
By another money-crazed fanatic
The only commercial that can heal your soul
Is not to be found in your cereal bowl
Buy yourself a book or a funny pet rat
It cracks me up it's as simple as that
Okay, it's time to wrap this up and go and get my coffee cup
Society is so insane and we're the prisoners of this game
Roll the dice, live in debt, and the running wheel is all you'll get
Addicts to addicts—dust to dust
We all must decide In What We Trust.

A Real Peace To Print

The newspaper said: I must condense
Be briefly sweet and less intense
They offered I could pay to be heard
Since they control the printed word
Then they confided as if to confess
They pay some writers who *will* say less!
Less of what's true but more to buy
These puppets of the Corporate Lie
Reality is, you're more apt to recall
A rhyming verse that'll break your fall
Editorials are much harder to repeat
Pass on to friends like a song to speak
What is it they don't want to show?
Poets defined this country you know?
Amazing Grace or 'Tis of Thee
You're slowly losing Miss Liberty
Stop the clocks and look around
Be the observer in this town
Demand less gossip and violent exposure
Stand up for peace in a loving composure
Enemy black blood smears like ink undried
Wash your hands of this cursed pride
The Judge and Jury shall not be US!
The Truth shall prevail in God I trust.

Invasion Of The Body Snatchers

Being a so-called citizen here
The old movie comes to mind:
'Invasion Of The Body Snatchers'
The best soul-stealing movie of all time
I live in NH yet not quite converted
There's so many potholes to be averted!
You'll look like a drunk navigating this Hell
For all of your efforts I have a story to tell
Driving with courtesy long ago was the rule
It's now the exception like staying in school
A yellow light means haul ass or wait Ten
More minutes that is, 'till it's your turn again
Just read our newspaper for a one-sided crime
Slamming one of their scapegoats every time
What about the landlords who'll suck dry your veins
Cause this is a college town with out-of-state gains?
Live free or DIE—our State license plate claims
While pedestrian zombies are dragging their chains
Step right out in front of you cause they're already dead!
Totally pointless thinking they'll get ahead
Or they're in a pick-up truck designed like a tank
Squeezing their big butts through a lane at the bank
Oh yeah speaking of *waiting* to see someone
Try the Emergency Room if you want to have fun
For hours on end you can gag into the air
Cause you're considered a fake for being there!
With these kind of people you're better off alone
They won't help you up much less toss you a bone
But there they are dressed up on a Sunday!
Then toting their guns come Glorious Monday
They cut you off and hiss at your presence
Look straight beyond the laboring peasants
You'll need antidepressants and sedatives to assist
Cause you'll get so disgusted and royally pissed
I could keep writing about all the Absurd
But you can ask any one of us who goes unheard.

My Body, My Soul

They say I have an attitude
The Pagans *so* disdain
I emphasize their tactics
Of twisting up your brain
One guy did a homicide
Another sold a joint
To an undercover nark!
Need I press this point?
The media is *their* servant
But won't work for you or I
We're supposed to question not
The reason for the Lie
Marijuana *is* less offensive
Adults to adults can choose
To relax, sit back and laugh
Or suck nicotine and booze
Don't you know 'their' motive?
Your health and mood are shot!
So you bicker with your family
Dividing House and Lot!
'They' push smokes and alcohol
Our anxiety pleads suppression
From the inner conflicts
Stemming from depression
You who never smoked an herb
Don't give me *your* debate
Untainted plants were put here
Before you Hypocrites of Hate
My Peace Pipe calls a "checkmate"
On your Bishop of Bullshit
Who said you could rewrite the Book?
You Judge *and* Hypocrite!
I'd rather retain my freedom
Than heed your hissing voice
I think adults are old enough
Their body is their choice.

God Don't Sell Trees

The Easter Bunny and the Undertaker
Sitting under a tree
S-M-I-L-I-N-G
First came the plan
Then came the lie
We're the ones who don't ask why.

Satan and Santa
Cutting down the tree
F-A-L-L-I-N-G
First came the deal
Then came illusion
Now we celebrate in confusion.

Uncle Sam and the Garbage Man
Selling plastic trees
D-E-C-V-I-N-G
First comes money
Then comes waste
Now in the mirror is a guilty face.

Vows Without Honor

The diamond was cursed
Beholden to the gold
It was inevitable from the start
The marriage would turn cold
She obsessed about the dress
His bow tie was so distracting
All those eyes upon their backs
While the priest was re-enacting
A fairytale he did recall
Before his solemn vow
To never make the same mistake
His father made somehow
All the secrets in the chapel
Were threatened to be exposed
When the bride decided to say "I don't"
And the sentence not imposed
Wisdom cannot be chained
Because of man's persistence
She knows too well about
His need for her existence
Yet he swears to keep her low
Within his mighty wall
She is not to be a slave
At his beckon call
Icy metal and cold stone
Does not a union bind
Nor some formal ritual
Etched inside the mind
Give her back her space
Don't rehash your Eden story
A woman does so represent
The power of God's Glory.

When Bad Does Good Beware

I could have been a donor to a little girl in need
Though it was a difficult day God urged me to proceed
The snowstorm kept on raging but the people stood in line
It was a beautiful vision and everything seemed fine
Still my daughter was quite heavy in my better arm
I didn't want to drop her and bring her to such harm
I inquired of a man orchestrating our positions
I told him I had a handicap that might hamper my decision
To stay or go I was now unsure so he ushered me inside
Where this tall blue-eyed man spat out at me so evilly and snide
He said "*We have* childcare! What *more* do you want!?
His tone was irked and rough, tongue lashed as if to taunt
I wasn't looking for a handout or a place to get ahead
I am not like him internally quite dead
I was all shaken up by this person I hadn't met before
Why was the Enemy in a church watching at the door?
Overwhelmed, I chose to leave but I *had* to ask his name
He hissed, "My name is *BF!*" as if I'd lost some game
He had *no* right in his stress to attack me for I *am* disabled
But because it's not as obvious he had me marked and labeled
Because of my limitation I had only sought to sit
I'd sit outside if it pleased him so had I even thought of it!
This poised angel of light with his tainted charity
Fear, Power, and Greed exposed himself to me
His Dealership is typical of the 'big name' Legion
They all run in packs in this dark Monadnock Region
Now again I'm asking God the purpose of it all?
A little girl needs each of us to hear her precious call
But Satan knows *no* boundaries when he uses men worn down
This is just another example of his Lordship in our town.

Not So Keene Winter

I woke up this morning
Looked out at the scene
My car was gone
And so was Keene!
Okay, who's the _____
Still praying for snow?
There's always Alaska
If you didn't know
Tote your boots
Goggles and skis
Go where it froze over
The disfigured trees
Snowmen and hot cocoa
A year 'round thrill!
I'll call you a plane
I'll pay the bill!
One more storm
I'll help you pack
We'll survive
If you don't look back
I made a bumper sticker
For your rear end
Live Freeze And Die
Goodbye dear friend
'Twas a Scenic place
No longer your home
Send us a postcard
When you reach Nome.

Inciters of Driven Rage

You get in your car
Life becomes chance
How many self-absorbed
Won't signal in advance?
G o   u l t r a   s l o w
Or light speed fast
Power-starved tailgaters
Up your ass
So you tip your mirror
Rather than react
To the Sociopath
Weapon at your back
Tanks obscuring view
Like generals in a war
All they lack is a swastika
Printed on their door
There's never a cop
To issue a stiff fine
To the Omega Man
Control-freak of the line
For every given license
There should be a class
And I don't mean a test
A monkey could pass
Three strikes could apply
To maniacs of the road
Who leave their house
Looking to explode
Sometimes you just pull over
Better yet turn around
Cause it only escalates
After mile two I found
God grant us to be patient
And keep us educated
That some so need a doctor
Who'll keep them medicated
The rules of the road
Will never apply to these
Until their wrongful right
Is taken with their keys.

Mental Trash

There it lay,
    run over,
        in the road.

I must look
At sweet fate
Stuck to tar

Translucent

    skin flutters

        in the breeze.

Ants gather
A happy
Eulogy

Apple pie,
    is no more,
        forgotten.

Mind Over Matter

What really is thin?
What is really fat?
Is he always the dog?
She in all ways a cat?
If they're in power
Why do they shake?
Does feeling pain
Cause one to break?
Do we have an anthem
Or just another poem?
When you escape a house
Did you run from home?
When we're up so high
Don't we look down?
If you try to remember
Are you apt to frown?
Paint too many rainbows
And it all turns black
So you fall to pieces
Yet you look intact
Oh why bother
Attempting to find
The thing that's lost
Is just your mind.

Seal Killers' Curse

Canada:
Red-spattered photos
Seals mercilessly bludgeoned
In front of each other
Hundreds of meek creatures
Ruthlessly beaten
To Death

Did the Almighty miss this too?
Is He at all grief-stricken
Are You?
Enraged enough
To curse
Greedy Men of Massacres?

Pray I, they too Suffer
Three-times this Fate

Abaddon! Abaddon!
Personification of Destruction!
Avenge Your Children now
Hear their cry of Pain
Blood on ice
Stained waters
Of Egypt
Refrain.

Societal Cage

A beautiful pregnant woman
Becomes the ugly single mother
Her ugly duckling
Will be a beautiful swan
So many beautiful cars
Are driven by ugly egos
An ugly self-interest
Can mar a beautiful charity
A beautiful body
Can harbor an ugly soul
The ugly indigent
May have a beautiful heart
A beautiful song
Can tell an ugly story
Ugly air pollution
Won't stop a beautiful sunset
A beautiful ocean
Can have an ugly shoreline
An ugly nightmare
Begs a beautiful daydream
The beautiful chapel
May hide an ugly truth
An ugly separation
Can bring beautiful solitude
A beautiful bouquet
Mocks an ugly funeral.

A Broken Heart
(In Memory of Jack the Cat)

You died
Suddenly they said:
A heart condition.
Deeply well I knew
The stagnant waters
Of your sadness
Days before we hugged
In the stunning spring sunlight
Our mutual weakness
Silently exposed
Eyes closed in
A preparatory parting
Another fallen sparrow
Is God too busy again?
Can I blame Him now?
Do I weep or scream?
For the meek inherit
Nothing in life
Just torment?
Like Christ died in pain
Believed He was forsaken
'Twas a broken heart.

Love Hate This State

New England weather
Empirically erratic
Polarized personas
Claim Democratic
Nothing expected
Is automatic
The gossip elicits
Too much static
Dare question why
I'm so emphatic
I stand in refusal
To be diplomatic
I've met too many
Psychosomatics
And gun-toting
Paranoid fanatics
Live free or die
A stupid politic
I'll gladly die free
Your hated heretic
Oh, Hypocrites of NH!
Hear me tell
Bigots and Liars
Whores that sell
Church-going Demons:
Fuck you
Farewell.

The Peace Prize

The Peacemaker
Complains not
Has no resentment
Nor is caught
By many-eyed spiders
Spinning webs of deceit
For those who might fall
Conceding defeat
No escape or attack
She forgives not forgets
The deluded disciples
Of hates and frets
She stays under the wing
Of the dove in De Light
Her aura most Divine
Unrequited to spite
Christ is still on a mission
Wipes scales from the eye
Of every Believer
Who questions not why
This Life be but Death
A Great Serenity Prayer
The ultimate journey
The Victor's career
She'll don no mask
But her armor is known
By the Enemy of Love
The money-fed Drone
When he stands accountable
With a flaccid forked tongue
All dissension shall cease
And Thy Kingdom come.

Everlasting Faith

In this dark world
Is the "She"
Living green earth
Wrapt 'round Her
She comforts
A Lonely Dove
Her heart pierces
Through Her Being
Crystalline channel
Upon her head
The birthmark
Of a fallen angel
Pleads guidance
Pleads strength
In this paralysis
Of Karmic belief
A lit candle
Reveals a silhouette
Both black
And luminous
Against the wall
Of existence
A faithful servant
Forever silent
Forever waiting
For everlasting.

I Remember

You love....and held
The one child who fell
Bloody knee, broken ego
He sobbed in your arms
I watched in sad silence
As you heal with a kiss.
All pains a part of life
But within My soul
A deep ugly scar
I always knew
Dear mother
You didn't
Love
Me
No hugs
No kisses
No Birth Days
No Good Nights
No... I cannot forget.

Name This Game

Simon says get off my ass
You follow much too close
But if that bus were not so slow
I'd not drive comatose
I knew I had a destination
Now forgotten where I'm going
Cause there's a yellow behemoth
Driving like he's mowing
Unseen fields in our path
For a never ending mile
I watch a kid pick his nose
I simply have to smile
Why are they looking at me
Like I'm the picture here?
They're the ones on an Edu-tour
That's taking them nowhere
You can study all you want
And never catch your dream
There's no diploma in this race
When the work is so extreme
Here is my report card
For the duck, duck and goose
For the hider and the seeker
Players of hangman's noose
Never forget to hula-hoop
Have a tea party with a friend
Let the witless win at checkers
It's more fun if you pretend
'Cause you'll be a scientist
A healer or a thief
You'll flip-flop in religion
And dispute your own belief
It's about time this guy
Does his tipping turn
Patience is a virtue
It matters what you learn.

Freeze Frame

Fat Rat and Slim Cat
Sitting by the road
Who'd you think shows up?
But Smartypants the Toad
He said "I have to cross.
Why do they go so fast?"
"I don't really care" said Slim
"It's amusing when they pass"
"My name's Bubba, this is Slim."
Said rat to Smartypants
"We're a couple of spectators
Of human circumstance."
"I'll see you later" said the Toad
"I have things that must be done.
I've not time to hang around
My life has just begun."
Like a skipping stone was he
Across the glittery gray mat
He never looked both ways
So now he's lying flat
Bub and Slim kept their secret
Of why they were together
A couple of philosophers
Discussing more than weather
When the traffic made no sense
To the point it did confound
The two just sauntered off
To the fringes of the town
I only mention this
'Cause every day's the same
Predictably we end up here
Like a photo in a frame.

Honor Withheld

I had a pet rat named 'Simon'
He'd fetch and knew his name
He never tried to bite me
Hide-and-seek was his best game

One day I saw his face inquire
Why some people hated his kind
Why did so many believe
The stories so well designed?
The flea passed out the plague
Hopped on other furry ones
We get no credit for research
Bred for science by the tons

We give our lives fighting cancer
Our wild cousins clean up trash
We're victims of the business
Of being fed to snakes for cash
Yet if only one would stop
And let the truth sink in
They'd see we're cleaner than cats
Smart as any dog within
We show affection and excitement
Just to see you walk in the room
And if you give us permission
Your fingers we would groom.
I could only look back at Simon
With much sadness in my eyes
Because so few in the human race
Will ever live above the lies.

Daughters Unite

If we obey every one
We shall crumble
Too many masters
Then we mumble
"Why me! Why me!
I've done my time
I am persecuted
Without a crime
Oh but to fail!"
Martyr without cause
Replay the message
Then actually pause
God gave you a Spirit
A Voice for to speak
A temple of Strength
The Wisdom to seek
A path of empowerment
The Courage to soar
A Name in His honor
Love needs not more
Stop playing the Victim
Redefine your role
Comfort each other
Or lay down your Soul
Destiny is yours
Submissive fear deny
Dear Father of Truth
Lift your Daughters on high!

"B" Is For ....

Beautiful butterflies
Balancing by botanical brilliance
Beside Bethlehem's broken boundaries

Bloodstained boulders
Behold bad bureaucracies
Bought by belligerent brutes
Bearing bayonets
Building barricades
Bursting bombs

Baffled bystanders besieged
Bartholomew beseeching
Brotherly blessings below

Beggars became boasters
Boding burdens beyond belief

Bewildered bodies bowing
Because battlefields bury bones
Bringing back bottled bereavements

Battered boys
Barren bosoms
Bitter brides

O' but beautiful butterflies
Balance by botanical brilliance
Bordering black-lined Bethlehem.

Mitochondria

Do not Undermine,
    Overshoot,
      nor Bad Rap

The Prophetess

Do not Lie to,
    Steal from,
      nor Betray

The Prophetess

Do not expect Anything,
    Everything,
      nor Nothing

Do not Look Back,
    Re-enter,
      nor Reminisce

She is the Omna
She is the Present
She is the Breath of Life

We are the Dust.

A Poet's Pendulum

When maple leaf clusters flutter
And wide lake waters shimmer
When mountain mica shines
And beach sands dazzle
I feel elation
However:

When hot pavement glitters
And littered cans glisten
When the peasant's brow shines
And weapons of war flash
I feel such sorrow
Still:

When the canopy of stars twinkle
And the morning dew glows
I feel blessed
Yet:

Tears sparkle and blur
My every vision.

Haiku IQ

Is this short enough
To print in the newspaper
Or is it too wrong?

Haiku Snafu

Why stifle poets?
Editorials drag on
No rhyme or reason

Snafu Haiku

Defining snafu:
Chaotic or confusing
American dream

Dolls Can't Dance

In this Valley of Dolls
A child was born
With life and vitality
And plenty of scorn
She looked and thought
A different way
So other parents
Warned stay away
Hence, happily
She played alone
Amongst the squirrels
And flowers grown
Why should she compete
To be shallow and cold?
Where is the freedom
Trapped in a mold?
Life is for dancing
Creating a song
No matter who listens
Or judges it wrong
Call her a stranger
What's that make you?
But the mirrored-image
Of a personal view
Plastic is dead
Duplication lives not
For imitation is suicide
In case you forgot.

Forgotten

I forgot to remember
You stole me a buy
To tell you the truth
They sold you a lie
I'm eighty-years young
Not a fool goes gray
I see black on white
Your night is my day
Your soul is imprisoned
You don't think for yourself
Cause you're wearing a leash
With your brain on the shelf
When you chose to borrow
A victim of the lender
Why should it surprise you
The Receiver is the Sender
Of every transgression
Blamed on the other side
While you stand on your hill
You're as low as your pride
If you think I'm inverting
The surreal-estate story
Tell me where in the cemetery
Are the riches and glory?
Headstones mark the same
You can't revoke what you said
While alive in your death
Why'd you consider me dead?
Now I'm alone but for God
No more lonely than before
Stuck in this wheelchair
Watching the door.

Dead Wrong For Right

Crusading for Christianity
Denouncing God's humanity
Confess, repent, baptismal bath
To save you from the coming wrath
I don't think there's a certain fix
Scripture is no bag of tricks
We all know who the other be
Raising Cain for democracy
Freedom fighters fight just that
Dropping civilians in their path
I met the Inquisition today
Condemning what I had to say
Hypocrites in rubber masks
Sipping from their holy flasks
As if they'll be hidden in the end
What goes around shall come again
Disobedience can be a gentle smile
While forced to walk in single file
I turn my cheek to see my Brother
Blood and bones of our Mother
She was judged by ruthless men
But Jesus shall lift her again
He'll call her name in the breeze
Set her broken heart at ease
Hand her a flashing sword of Light
Redeem her children from the night
Winged woman be like a dove
Shrewd as the Snake of worldly love
Behold the day is drawing so near
But Lady Wisdom can't make you hear
If you don't listen nor believe it so
Tell me where do dead men go?

Metamorphosis

M-alevolent Medusa
E-ncapsulates Evil
T-error turns to
A-bsolute Anxiety

    (her black eyeliner never runs)

M-aking Madness
O-ut of Order
R-edefining Reality
P-ermeating Pain
H-allucinogenic Horror
O-vertaking Outsiders
S-erpents swirling

    (like steel painted fingertips)

I-nvading idle
S-enses.

To Love or Perish

We live in a numb Society
We are taught not to cry
But to act 'Professional'
When we see a creature die
We elect a judge to execute
Condemn those to the chair
Who refuse to be Conformists
To that which is not fair
"All men are created equal"
Said the master to his slave
Took the harvest for himself
While preaching Christ forgave
Such sins of fallen angels
Who like to publicly repent
Then privately plan retribution
For those who might dissent
Cut down or burn the bush
With ornamental fruit
It tempts the starving soul
Renders all believers mute
Go to your neighbor's door
Comfort them not to hide
Only fear can lock a house
Holding prisoners inside
Summon all of your children
Hypnotized and in a trance
Every life should matter
Regardless of circumstance
They televise great violence
Distort-Report the facts
Hoping to break your Spirit
Leave no Will or Hope intact
I may write a word of sorrow
For the Planet with no friend
But environments need healing
So God's Love can live again.

O' To Love Once More

I am in love
With a part of you.
The side of your heart
Still yearning and wanting
To be loved for who you are.
I'll comfort the half that remains.
If it is all you have to give right now.
I was not to witness when she was there,
Wielding her knife of impossible standards
Like the Queen of Spades dealing by desire.
Truly envy is ignorance—imitation suicide.
Yet you tried to please with every ounce:
Beg, borrow and steal for her to but see
You gave from the veins of your Soul.
But it would never ever be enough.
Your ache now a silent scream.
Nightmare-ridden dreams
Became a hemorrhage.
Necrosis set in hard.
To be reabsorbed
Into emptiness
To a void
The next
Time

O'

Defining the Terror 'Ism'

The American Heritage Dictionary: n.
"The political use of violence or intimidation."

Torturing	traveling	temperamental
Evil	enigmatic	enemies:
Relaying	retaliatory	rationales,
Reinforcing	religious	resentments,
Over	opaque	omnipotent
Royally	righteous	radicals
Inducing	isolated	ideological
Sovereign	symbolism:	statistically
Maintaining	myopic	madness

Note: Before you judge this work, carefully study the definitions of *each* word as applied.

Autumn Calls

This poem is about a beloved hooded pet rat who was loved dearly by many who met her.

Autumn Calls: Dedicated to "Oreo"

Prolonging Death is hardly kind
When all is lost but for the mind
If you had been there to suffer long
You'd see that Medicine is truly wrong
The eyes of Love beg let me go
My dress fades glorious as you know
Cry but a moment then sigh relief
For I am free
          the autumn leaf.
                    I spiral down

The breeze my friend
Back to the earth to rise again
I'll be the robin, the sun and tree
The season claims my Destiny
This captive Soul may you release
Your understanding brings me Peace.

Is This Life Death?

What did I do?
What did I say?
Am I that ugly?
Am I too gray?
Is it that obvious
The people I hate?
It is only for those
Who force me to wait
But here is my poem
A psalm you won't sing
Only God's animals
Care what I bring
To this earth all alone
A stranger I have been
Although I keep trying
I fail all over again
Where can I hide
My daughter protected?
From all that is Evil?
From Ones so infected?
I'd purge all possessions
I'd fast every day
If only I could find
The True and Right Way
Out of this mess
Out of this skin
Out of this World
They have made me live in
But for the flowers
The squirrels having fun
My beautiful sky
The trees praising Sun
I'd be in despair
Every minute—every breath
Will somebody tell me
Is my Life really Death?

Lamentality

I didn't come here to win
I didn't come without sin
I fell and that's my fate
So you go on and guard that gate
I'm going nowhere 'til I hear a voice
Calling my name above the noise
I'm ready to go when it is my time
Too long I've been grounded for a crime
There was never forgiveness on this path
God forever has engaged His wrath
I'm tired of all this negative shit
All these zombies without a wit
Never shall I be one of them
Don't ever drop me here again!

Dedication to Mrs. Hallahan:

If going home is an alcove of Peace
Then shed thy skin and Soul release
A body can fail but not our Love
The memories be like Noah's Dove
And when we come to understand
Grief withdraws its crippled hand
When Life is burdened in the end
Death is known The Welcome Friend
Forever blessed for what you taught
Shine my Star, forget-you-not.

Curse Enemy Mine

For all the tarnish on that silver lining
For all the small print when I was signing
If not for bad luck the word wouldn't exist
I've been the moving target on someone's list
No wonder I had to double-lock the doors
Watch my every step on those glossy floors
The moment I looked up the Enemy was there
A smirk on his face and his mate with a sneer
Why God did not slay those gossips and witches?
Or lay their carcasses into unmarked ditches?
Those lustful dumb men longing to rape my Soul?
Those self-righteous neighbors so brutal and cold?
From this moment on I petition the Thunder
Note every Intruder and slash them asunder
So much as a thought of ill-will sent my way
Oh Master of Elements make them pay
I reclaim my Power and Daughter as well
Threaten either of us and you shall taste Hell
Old Testament Angel shall crush your pride
Thrust and twist Her sword in your side
My punishment is done as my youth is gone
I'm the harmless old woman with a deadly song.

Skeletons in America's Closet

You best be damn careful if you are poor
Don't anger the neighbor or knock on his door
Don't call the police or they'll haul YOU away
Never get sick and need a hospital stay
You are despised and blamed for your lot
Condemned to poverty, lest you get caught
Court-appointed lawyers will get you big time
Until you accept being born was your crime
You'll never matter come floods or fire
You're not a viable citizen like those who retire
That kind of American is now useless and frail
So they create "nursing homes" to put you in jail
The elder torture chambers are rather well known
But not the botched records that confiscated your home
Oh yes, those *HOMELESS*, I had almost forgotten
Considered the worst of low-life and rotten
They'll give out their aid, but not without a fight
Call you "assertive bitch" standing up for what's right
I know this mark in this Predator's Game
Spread all of that gossip of how I'm insane
Now that is the worst, having mental health attacked
A little depression will get you totally whacked
With no credibility, you're ordered to stand down
Take their legalized tranquilizers or leave this town
Uh huh, this is our country and it is all true
Ask most single mothers—oops!—it's their fault too!
Well sooner or later the pendulum shall swing
'We all fall down' I heard the caged bird sing.

Reduce Speed: Life Zone

When I see them lying on the side of the road
My heart startles for a split second, then I pull back
Into myself with utter sadness—to die this way.
My eyes often well up while I'm driving in my own car.
Have you ever once lay down next to your car
Looked over at those tires, the rubber smells hits you,
As you look under and up at the beast you must tame.
A luxury for you that can kill in a split second.
What horror could you deny?
And the humble merely wish to cross over
As they prepare for the coming winter.

I often go back to that still silhouette
Curled up so precious and often still formed
Asleep I like to imagine.
I don't care what the other drivers think
Or don't think.
I've learned after forty-years that it only matters
Someone take responsibility, if not the killer.
With care and dignity return that smaller being to the earth.
With prayer, blessings and apologies:
From the human race that knows no speed limits.

Angels Go Crazy

Angels go crazy
It's no surprise
Expected to start life
The moment it dies
Arms where once wings
Feet where were none
Halos taken up
By the burning Sun
Auras of friction
Humans despise
Fallen Empire
In darkened eyes
We tend to look up
Aware of our fall
Once Universal
Now terribly small
Quite insignificant
It is a notion to be
Cast in dead flesh
Like the Enemy
God lift Your wrath
Forgiveness ours too
Creation imperfect
Our sentence undo
We're not of this world
Hear our cry now
We are ostracized beings
Of this broken vow
Petitioners we unite
Give up our possessions
Lift us on high
Excuse our digressions
We praise you and sing
Bow in your Name
Jehovah or Allah
The eternal flame.

In Memory of a Brown Rat Named Reebok

I knew of eleven Innocents, their little Souls put down
Never had a chance in life for a family to be found
They grew up in the chaos of assaulting noise and light
No one took the time to see these beings of the night
I came along all too late when their fate was all but sealed
So many unfairly hated them as though they couldn't feel
Have a mind or precious dream God gifted every creature
Perfected only in animals this unconditional feature
All too ready to give you love and trust our two-legged kind
Sniffing for the safe one because some are very blind
Never prejudiced toward us and all too ready for you to play
'Til a human came along and snatched that trust away
Now terror-stricken he bit that familiar poking hand
Could it be the same one of the last malevolent man?
I've seen the rat nine painful years, a hundred come and gone
And the fear of these domestic ones is ab-so-lute-ly wrong
Despising their tails is likened to judging a friend by limb
This will be part of our extinction as the ultimate Living Sin
Thou shalt not kill nor euthanize based on ignorant data bases
And our inhumane society shall be haunted by those faces.

Powerless Power

Have you met the Devil 'He-She'?
With severe aquiline features?
She's poised on every pinnacle
Extolling all her preachers
She dances quite seductively
In a body starved for power
Her lips a pursed and cynical grin
For the next victim to devour
She infiltrates all institutions
Vilifies the loving measure
Befriends unwitting foes
All souls for short-lived pleasure
She knows I know her in a room
My Angel 'tween us silent
I'm the poet she's come to hate
My verse is non-compliant
My hair, blood and falling tears
Have been noted by the Sun
I have given everything
Now Thy will be done
This shall be her kingdom
Blue-black planet lost in space
A floating grave of ill-repute
Banished in disgrace
So Miss Lady of Disguise
And Mr. Debonair
You're a CEO nothing
Except ultimate despair.

Anonymous Author: Revised

We the unwitting
Led by the unknowing
Are trying to do the impossible
For the ungrateful.

We have done so much
For so long
With so little
That we are now qualified
As slaves
To do nothing
About anything.

A Poet's Chore

We are like the dinosaur
No one sees us anymore
Our pterodactyl metaphor
You've but chosen to ignore
Like victims of an unseen war
You're hiding out behind a door
But all the Gods are keeping score
What was shall be as was before
And all the poets apiece implore
But peace cannot begin to roar
While every dollar has its whore
Slaves to scrub the Master's floor
His pitcher full of souls to pour
He's a greedy collecting connoisseur
And so we grieve the lonely poor
On their island from our shore.

A Rational Anthem

In our heart of hearts
We know, we know
We come around
Around we go
Spinning wheels
Spinning tires
Spinning thoughts
On spinning spires
We wonder why
I ask, why wonder?
They've spun the spell
You've been put under
Drugged and numb
In an addict's attic
Remote in hand
You crave the static
You live in the current
Of this current existence
Would never question
One man's persistence
In a losing game
Of love and hate
We hate to love
Predestined fate
Now entertain
This final thought
Could we be lost
If found we're not?

The Conduit

One cannot plan the process
Of a poem
No more than a pregnancy
A literal gestation period
Riding the swells
Of good words
In bad worlds
And bad words
In good worlds

In the background therein
Beats a rhythmic cadence
Both furious and eloquent
Muffled by layers
Of muscle and fat

It bifurcates off the writer
A living conduit
Rendered silent

Validated only when she
Can name the body
With a title.

Angels We Have Heard On High

'So this is Christmas...
And what have you've done?'
Does anyone recall
The song Lennon had sung?
'For the rich and the poor ones
For the black and the white'
For the humble disabled
Warm or cold on this night.
I would extend it to the Earth
Our pets and the Sun
To the wind-beaten Postman
To the long rivers that run
To the innocent child
And the elderly Soul
To the Givers of Love
And the Hands that fold
'A very Merry Christmas
And a Happy New Year'
No matter the weather
Try to be of good cheer
Each of us encounters
A box of burdens to bear
And only through Peace
Can we vanquish the Fear
'Another year over
A new one begun'
The Messenger is near
She calls every one.

Lore of the Flies

Science won't say you're the pig and rat
Or why some people adore an arrogant cat
Don't get this wrong, there's infrequent exceptions
Like when the media tells a Truth within the deceptions
Psychologists can't say that your curly-haired friend
Is brighter than you with your hidden rear end
How we're taught to hide 'cause Barbie is Queen
Compromising to fit in is to Self really mean
Corporations lure poor ones to shop 'til they sweat
Their illusion of success is to be living in debt
They plan to retrain you and modify that degree
With all of their policies you'd have to agree
Pretend to say grace when Religion is King
Of the psyche and shell—what Spirit *could* sing?
So gorge—imbibe—and act merry
A Gossip carries The Plague
And when there's no trust
Your Contract is vague
Best know and love your neighbor
Don't decide you have a Class
We are all in this together
To Them, (hello?), we are trash
Smile at Them and obediently nod
Meanwhile stand ready for the vengeance of God.

Democracies Defy Dictatorships

Dictators deliberately design disasters.
Deviant derelicts direct deranged delegates
During desperate dark days.
Depraved dangerous dragons
Delightfully doublespeaking
Deuteronomy divinely denounces
Dollar-driven desecrations.

Don't delay!
Disdain despotic demagogues.

Defenseless deaf dumb dolls dine drunkenly.
Dull dormancy detains dust.
Dogs die digging dirt-delivered dreams.
Dissolve delusions divisively daring doubt.

Declare deception deceased.
Do defiantly dance.
Democracies defy Dictatorships!

"I" Is For....

Incorrigible Ivan
Interfering in Iraq,
Insistently insulting internal intelligence:
Insidious intervention.
Invariably idiocy invokes illogical idioms
Instilling idiopathic illness.
Implying international interests inane.
Impulsive intimidation is illicit,
Illiberal, ill-mannered involvement.
Irate iconoclasts improperly institute
Independence.
Incensed insurgents implosively indulge
Injudicious intercession.
Ironically I iterate indelible insight:
Idle individuals impose isolating imprisonment
Irresponsibly impervious.
Is impeachment inevitable?

War Mangled Manner

O' how can you see
If your lids are sewn shut?
How so proudly we failed
To read our Pre-si-dent's mean-ing
Whose intentions unclear
And a mind not quite there
Or the news that we saw
Was so gallantly seeming

But the clusters bombs fell!
Oil rivers would swell!
And the angels stood back
From this Christian-led hell

O'say did those children
Put up a—big—fight
When you top-pled their homes
On that cold dead-ly night.

Lead Us by Example

The troops see terror
With each rising sun
We must pray for peace
Send support to each one
They must do the job
Because they enlisted
Who ever knew defense
Could become so twisted?
God bring them home safely
From a tour of great sorrow
Wait not another day
We've witnessed tomorrow
The continual bloodshed
Crying mothers in black
That last kiss goodbye
They can never take back
It's an endless futile course
Not full of old glory
We are being shamed
For this tragic story
As in Vietnam
We suffered similar gains
We gave no real honor
Just listed their names
Crippled or dead
In a losing war
I bow my head
I ask, what for?
Freedom you say?
By who's definition?
For each individual
It's a private transition
Liberty is not just
A physical thing
That's why the caged bird
Continues to sing
Who are we to decide
For every human being?
The Truth is quite evident
For believing is seeing.

Blind As A Bat Fallacy

You ever stopped long enough
To watch a bug on its mission?
Are you even allowed
To make such a decision?
Before you stigmatize
The smallest life form
Watch what they're doing
In spite of the storm
Huge feet and poisoning
Wiped away with a crumb
Thrown in the trash
Into the toilet go some
    Okay—now take the dog
He's harder to throw away
How much do you miss him
As he does you every day?
Show me a person as loyal
Minds their own business
Keeps all of your secrets
Gossips not your existence
Review now the rodent
Is he really a criminal rat?
Anymore than would be
Your pampered fat cat?
Have you owned such a critter?
This miniature dog in disguise?
Actually better stated: a human
Untainted by pride?
The point in this matter
The Kingdom is in your midst
Pay attention and see it
Such perfection exists.

The Eyes of Love

When our pets leave us
They may come around
In a spiritual form
This I have found
For in my dream
Monty came back
Tho' I couldn't see him
He made pointed contact
He let me know clearly
This is how it would be
Without physical vision
We'd be able to see
Death kills not Love
As it shall patiently wait
Times passes quickly
Tho' sorrow seems great
The Kingdom be restored
The animals always knew
They try to show us the Way
The Book of Thomas is true
And for every human touched
By these Angels of Light
There's celebrating in Heaven
When that Soul does take flight
Out of the body of bondage
Go the heart and Old Soul
Eyes of Love pass wide open
As Jesus foretold.

Time in A Bottle

Do you love me
Or is it her?
The way we are
Or the way we were?
You alter your face
And then you yell
It's a wonder how
I took it so well
You demand recall
Like a priest in church
I stand composed
Yet frenetically search
When did I offend thee?
I'm failing so faint
Where are the angels?
Where is my saint?
I'm all alone here
I'm bleeding fast
Where is the door
Out of this past?
I'll shut my eyes
This ocean's deep
I drown in pain
I fall asleep
Do you hate that
Or is it this?
Tell me now
Does time exist?

Pending Divorce

You see color—I see blood
You claim rain—I claim flood
You feel power—I feel defeat
You think trust—I think deceit
You speak English—I speak verse
You say gift—I say curse
You seem mobile—I seem still
You guard slaves—I guard God's Will
You ask for war—I ask for why?
You hear no choice—I hear decide
You sing heroics—I sing unheard
You give excuses—I give the Word
You taste of power—I taste of Divine
You offer vinegar—I offer wine
You act carnal—I act insane
You profess cure—I profess pain
You be a man—I be a She
You be you—I'll be me.

Ten American Greevlings

"10" little greevlings standing in a line
One was "a person of interest"
Then there were "9".
"9" little greevlings in a debate
One was a Republican
Then there were "8".
"8" little greevlings claiming there's a Heaven
One got mega-sued
Then there were "7".
"7" little greevlings lighting candle wicks
One was a (can't say the "word" anymore)
Then there were "6".
"6" little greevlings playing war with knives
One got impaled
Then there were "5".
"5" little greevlings behind a locked door
One was an "informant"
Then there were "4".
"4" little greevlings just couldn't agree
One called the President
Then there were "3".
"3" little greevlings standing by you
One was afraid to fart
Then there were "2".
"2" little greevlings sitting in the sun
One asked about "global warming"
Then there was "1".
"1" little greevling yearned for another
Illegally cloned himself
Then there were others.

This is with thought about the Iraq war that seems more problematic than problem-solving. So much killing like a vicious unstoppable cycle so I wish our government hadn't so vengefully initiated for ulterior motives, it now seems.

Cancer Begins With "C"

Coercively compounding conformity
Coincidentally, condemns Christian concepts.

Concurrently, concerned communities
Could contract connections
Codifying commonality,
Creating conscientious control,
Contrasting catatonic coexistence.

Candidly castigate covert conspiracies
Conclusively costing casualties.
Cloaked camera-carrying crows
Collect confusing commentaries.

Consider courageous countries
Cohesively correcting colossal criminality
Congress cannot control.

Complacent compliance
Constitutes condoning corruption.

Ownership Has Its Price

Hamsters, gerbils, rats and mice
Who can really set the price?
Iguanas, turtles, snakes or fish
What kind of child has this wish?
Kitties, puppies, cats and dogs
Why not content just watching frogs?
Chinchillas, rabbits, ferrets or pigs
Spiders living in some twigs
I wonder if God so designed
The being of possessive mind
Every creature was meant to roam
Not force-bred and taken home
Creation is there but to see
The living earth in harmony
I too thought I owned my pet
So I write this lest I forget
I am here as brief it is known
From start to finish I have grown
And if I stop and contemplate
You might say I am running late
How absurd this stagnant race
Thinking it owns time and space.

The Aftermath

"One, to, free, for, five"
(Iraqi women's lives?)
My daughter next to me
Can't say the number three
Knows not my preoccupation
Swirling words in combination
Amidst the tension beating low
All around as if we know
A table turns as a tide will shift
This race is not just to the swift
Alignment of Spirits taking place
The worn out look on every face
We're being called to be as One
The real Revolution has just begun
Some do whisper, some carry signs
Some write cursive bitter lines
Black on white is what it takes
To rectify this big mistake
Passive stand in complacent fashion
Offers but a slave-wage ration
Ready or not 'cause here they come
Talking at you like you're dumb
Better yet, their sleeping fool
Remote in hand with mouth a-drool
Stop accepting this head game beating
The lies and circles are not quite meeting
Six, seven, eight, nine, and ten
It's basic math this tragic end.

Rumble in the Jungle

Reduce, share, unplug the fear
Or you haven't got a prayer
Hypocrites are everywhere
Speak your mind if you dare
Give not into weak despair
Call the Lion from his lair
His is not to really care
For the children far and near
See the smoldering Teddy Bear?
Not so far from here to there
Smoke does cloud the hemisphere
Yet we persist to blindly stare
Lacking the wisdom to prepare
Lose our shirts and underwear
Is that the power we revere?
A hateful greedy overseer
Sets the trap and snaps the snare?
His tactic is to create a scare
So you've no choice but to adhere
His Wolf makes speeches debonair
For sheep to slaughter so sincere
Collecting souls is his career
So hence we do not once declare
The double talk remains unclear
For what is there left to compare
But to be alive is to be aware.

Dictatorships

Divisive
Intrusive
Covert
Tactics
Americans
Think
Offer
Reasonable
Security
Holds
Individual
Prisoners
Submissive.

What Goes Around Comes Around

When it all comes out in the wash
She'll try to come running back
Placating me with a phony smile
As if my memory I would lack
She'd be the very last
I would ever offer again
My honest heart and openness
A trusted and loyal friend
Back down you Silver Viper!
I remember your Evil Name
I remember all my heartache
From your gossip and head games
Your accident is self-designed
I'll neither laugh nor gloat
But I'd admit it was about time
You left that suicide note
Now my every prayer is for the weak
And the victims you've left to die
The creatures you ran over
Even every swatted fly
Say what you want about me
I petitioned on you long ago
I have strong faith in Karma
God's Vengeance as you know
I may lack glorious wings
But this Spirit takes to flight
I watch you in your dreams
I shadow you every night
Dare you feign your innocence
The Universe shall cast you down
And no one will ever notice
When your Soul cannot be found
You're the prisoner and guard
Standing divided sad
You should have been a good girl
When you opted to be bad.

Televicious Transference

Televising trauma thoroughly
Encapsulates evil exposure,
Lucidly leveraged, locking
Every eye engaged
Victim—voiceless—volatile
Inducing idle isolation
Sending spirits spiraling
Into impoverished isolation
Only offering obsessive
Needless negative neuroses.

Stop Beating around the Bush

He's a terrorist just as those others be
I say the following in support of anarchy:
He ordered the reckless bombing
Of children and their mothers
He's the wolf in synthetic sheepskin
Surrounded by his Brothers
It is Unamerican to still
Support this murderous man
He's only wreaked destruction
Since his term began
Only a brown-noser
Would applaud his latest speech
The rest of US are mumbling
Overthrow him or impeach
This first Beast and friends
Will cause a nuclear war
Our men are getting massacred
What exactly for?
It's time to revolt
Since re-voting didn't work
He's rigged the electoral process
Now the media is berserk
Just as in 1776
It was the real 'Patriotic Act'
Americans could separate
His fiction from the fact
We know why We got bombed
Can you really not see the reason?
Try questioning your Government
It's now denounced as treason
A body of power that tortures
Steals and conjures lies
Then says this is Democracy
So psuedo-civilized
Bounced checks and balances
Have gotten out of hand
Take back your beloved country
Take back your 'give a damn'
"This cadence will be known
To preserve the Constitution
In my time the nursery rhyme
Will spark the Revolution."

Playing with the good old sayings you hear or say frequently and making sense of some of the senseless jibber jabber. This writing was actually fun. Occasionally, I try very hard to lighten up my verse. I just don't like phony come-on poetry that condescends on my fellow readers. It amazes me how few poets really speak to me as a person on the level of earthen plane. I do however appreciate those who can turn a leaf into such a big phenomenon. Well, it is. I can dig that too.

A Muse Among Us

A little sliver on a cold silver spoon
A little white lie a moment too soon
That takes the cake but never the pie
Do it over again but not sure why?
A dirty rat can make a clean getaway
Such ignorant bliss in all that you say
Once in a blue moon you do think twice
Wish upon a star when you roll the dice
Think about four eyes behind the eight ball
It was ten against one brick in the wall
But she got even and started to play rough
Told you umpteen times enough was enough
Like you never picked your nose or a fight
Now you can't change a bulb but can fly a kite
I don't walk on eggshells in a pretty glass house
Never throw stones or play the mute mouse
O' hickory dickory why do you watch the clock?
We know so much but can't walk the talk
What's so damn funny is you can't be serious?
You're reading this like it's mega-mysterious
To add insult to injury you cart the old horse
Say I'm out of my mind but not ask your source
Why is it called a Plural when it's only one Word
How can your hear but never have heard?
You parked your mouth and left it running today
It's a waste of my time and redundantly gray
Like the river that rages through the winter snow
Back to the ocean like some big league pro
I'll break all of the rules but never my neck
You're a slave labor fool who gets a stacked deck
Oops, it's shift change again to let the dog out
Do you know this game beyond a reasonable doubt?

A working off the letter "P", and again I'm pulled into the skaky conditions regarding the Iraq invasion by our President. Who put this to a vote with "The People"? I think "We The People" have about had enough. As for you "sleepers, self-medicated, and disillusioned" People, all of this will affect you and yours as well. Wake up call.

Poor Prognosis

Powerful persons
Posing poignantly proper
Present pragmatic propaganda.
Patriarchal political pachyderms
Propose preposterous policies
Preventing positive progress.
Pompous pagans preside
Praising pickpocket pawns.

Peasants penitently pray
Petitioning peaceful possibilities.
Punitive police post patriotic profiles
Promising punishment.

Pakistan presages poisonous
Permanent polarized perceptions
Pointing past
Previous pitfalls.

Pessimistic prophets predict
Pending pandemonium:
Pillaging, perversion, patrols,
Pestilence, parasitic proliferation,
Plagues, prevailing poverty.

Prognosis poor.

What Makes A Poet Laureate?

The Poet Laureate said to me:
So out of vogue is rhyme
As for meeting you my dear
I hardly have the time
The newspaper may have said
So much of me to flatter
As if I'd hear a stranger poet
Such caring doesn't matter
My post is quite political
I had to tap every contact
So the Governor approved
My status under contract
I'm not a Dickinson at all
But a Plath be all of you
Thinking you'll gain audience
By emoting what is true
The reality is sweetly bitter
I've more vital things at hand
I am crowned with a grand title
You would hardly understand
So go buy your Poet's Market
Your turn to grovel, beg or steal
My importance so overrides
Such weakness as to feel
For you a separate piece
A struggling writer unknown
You did nothing to put me here
Now go away leave me alone.

Grim Side of the Story

He handed me an hour glass
Turned it over in my palm
Told me "Have no fear
Release anxiety, be calm.
For all that you went through
We fast forward and rewind
This is where you always are
Living Death is all you'll find.
You sleep to dream and wake
The clock spins twice around
You end up where you started
A seed back in the ground.
Transmigration is a journey
Evolving with the earth
Welcome every chance
To redesign your birth."
I asked the Reaper why to sow
With a scythe as if to scare
Covered in black as a skeleton
The ghost of all despair?
He said, "Untrue be this myth
Like many so made up
Look here and see the rainbow
At the bottom of my cup!
In my right hand is this goblet
A spiritual drink not mentioned.
Close your eyes and look again
At the Separatist Invention
I take you all religious or not
Well or sick, old or young
The only sin is creating Gods
Confining every One
Unification is the circled secret
The Uni-verse but contains
When all is said and done
Love is what remains."

Whether or Not

Winter thunder
Summer haze
Ever wonder
In these days?

Major storming
Flooding zones
Global warming?
Aching bones?

On our knees
They strip land
They oil seas
We raise our hand

A playground quakes?
A ferocious wind?
The glacier breaks
The melt begins

Graying visions
A tsunami sent
Our decision?
Or the President?

Stop his killing
Stop his war
God be willing
We'll do more.

In Loving Memory of the Lily

I deeply care:
To the detriment
Of my own heart
(So they say)
Would I have it
Any other way?
I suppose not.

For as an angel shall walk
With me into the Light
I will walk with these
The meekest,
Most vulnerable,
Beings.

Time hurts and time heals
It is time that shall tell my heart
When I have concluded
A journey well done
A mission embraced
For better or worse
Selfless and giving
Honorable and kind

Suffer not
My dear Companion
I remain with you
And you with me
As Death cannot part
This loving heart.

Always A Poet

Sometimes a poet
Has to speak
What you don't
Want to hear.

Sometimes a poet
Uplifts the meek
When you won't
Give a prayer.

Always a poet
Stands alone
When they sit
And write.

Always a poet
Longs for home
Only to submit
At night.

Osix-Osix-Osix

The number game June six-o-six?
Encouraged events or another trick?
Masks and gloves be for the sick,
Sixty candles cut down the wick.
Batteries, toilet paper, food and gas,
Lots of water and plenty of cash.
Extra soap for hands and clothes.
Comes martial law no one knows.
The flu, the weather, a terrorist dream?
The time is near so it would seem.
Know your loved ones and where to hide.
Be wary of strangers bought on a bribe.
Have maps and firearms if you must run.
If you're a minority you'll be a targeted one.
Mr. Bush can't stay under ground.
They'll toss him out a wasted clown.
The media could end this nasty war.
Or take aim and focus a little more.
We've seen his politics not so nice.
Talk to each other now or pay the price.

Postal Prostitute

Though he be divorced
He is bound by a vow
For better or the worse
Death does what now?
Demon woman so thin
Your hair is a nest
Your conniving sin
Is getting undressed
Like an unwanted whore
Our government did employ
You slither 'cross the floor
Your dismissal I'll enjoy
For you treated me
Like a threat to your game
All I can ever see
Is a bitch with no name
I refuse to ever love
This viper from hell
God up above
I shall never tell.

Earth Heart Broken

Salutary sunrises
Rolling rivers
Open oceans
Majestic mountains
Hallowed hills
Greenest grass
Tallest trees
Free flowers
Refreshing rains
Royal rainbows
Beautiful birds
Wondrous wildlife
Serene sunsets
Stunning stars
I shall deeply miss you.

Thus, the malevolent men
The wizards of war
Have raped this planet
Of plenty...
    of pulse...
        of peace.

As he were space-born
So shall he return
Ever so lovelorn.

A-Z Mysteries

Absolute belief can deliver
Beauty. Concurrently, deceptive evil
Conveys destiny empirically fated.
Divine entities fortify glorious
Energy: friends give hearts
Freely gliding higher. Isis
Gives honorable insight jubilantly.
Humbly, I juxtapose Kings,
Insensitive Judges killing Life.
Justice kisses lost men,
Knows listless mermaids navigating
Loveless. Memory never opens
Mankind needlessly. Oceans passively
Nurture overcast painful quietude.
Our personal quest rocks
Paradise quintessentially. Rising suns
Quell restlessness. Shading trees
Resistant. Sorrow torments uttered
Solutions temporarily unifying vespers.
Truly unnatural voluminous wisdom
Underestimating violent willful xenophobes.
Vengeful wars, xeric years.
Willful Xenophanes yearns zazen
Xerographic Yin zeniths,
Yang zodiacal
Zaxes.

A Clinic Cynic

Does 'not too bad'
Mean 'not too good'?
I asked the doctor
If she really could
Explain such little
Evasive terms
Do I or don't I
Have killer germs?
The insurance company
Told you to be sure
Or there'd be no payment
For the needed cure.
I waited five days
For a "virus" you know
Why even go in?
Let those bacteria grow!
So here we are later
My lungs mock a seal
I cough up nothing
But this weak appeal:
Dear Higher Courts
Must only poor people die?
When will you stop allowing
This medical reply?
If you harm my child
I'll pluck your bones
Leave you for dead
Covered in stones
I'll petition the Angel
I'll circle your grave
Dome in your soul
As Satan's slave.

Ten Little Indians

I've seen the Indians
They came for their land
The rivers and trees
The mountains and sand
Sometimes they're in pairs
But more often alone
We've been so busy
How could we have known?
Money distracts US
The television attacks
Our conscience of care
Our knowledge of facts
O' dear 'sleepers'
Desensitized ones
Drugged and obsessed
Hiding your guns
The time has come
Warnings are gone
I'm with whom I love
With only my song
As it was in the beginning
It is now so in the end
I hope that I did well enough
To soar the skies again.

Why the Fat Lady Sings

Where is the sin in being fat or thin?
Live and let live, all treasure within
I am not plastic, nor claim fantastic
To freeze in a frame, a Soul to claim
This temple is mine, with a Self of Divine
I am not prized, for an ass and thighs
See a cut from a-torn and acknowledge her scorn
The female is much more than a physical score
While Hollywood lies, true happiness is not size
The extremes of control, reap sorrow—behold!
She is not some whore, for the richer or poor
Note smile and esteem, real laugh and a dream
A voice speaking song, yet maternally strong
Her heart be true and shall honor you
Her arms are home, not caustic bone
Brown eyes you admire, close enough for desire
For all women need space, to read your face
When she asks, is it okay, you will humbly say:
Dear ladylike Dove, now I truly do know Love.

Walking Out of the Womb

The canopy of night covers the land
The stars of heaven blur hand in hand
I drift to slumber and die again
I'm light as air
I drop my pen.

The moon defines a lit circle of birth
Death shall deliver each Soul from earth
I hope next time when I fly beyond
I'll become a gazelle or bird of song.

I can't seem to detach much more than an hour
Without being pulled back for my shell to devour
A prisoner of flesh I dream of ascension
I pray for peace in that dimension.

I'd write in blood if it would set me free
But my daughter whispers:
"I'm only three."
(A Mayan Doctor did not deliver
Us from the torrent of the river.)

O' dear Sky Dove, I'll stay for you.
I brought here,
I'll see you through.
And if I cry
It's so I'll wake again
And hold the Light
Until you can.

An Empty Bottle

Here I sit
Now clearly see
The fate of my efforts.
The ocean beats against this rock
Like swells and exhalations
Of a watery Beast
Furious that I am still
On the cliff
Legs dangling
Tauntingly
Or so it thinks.

Always the wind blows
Against me
From the left—then the right
In my face it forces salty tears
I refuse to give freely.
From behind it gives
An unfriendly shove.

Only at low tide
In the calm of sunset
I can lift the large quartz
From my stack of paper.
My finger traces invisible words
While the water knowingly waits
For the falling one
To land softly on its surface,
Eager to toss it to and fro
Until it obediently sinks
Wordless and forgotten.

Another message
Out of the bottle.

The Statue of Mary

I drive Congress Street
Like a regular trail.
I see palms turned up
In a powdered-blue veil.
This woman leans forward
As if to appeal:
Lift this heavy stone
My arms are too frail.
Now she stares at the ground
With tears to conceal
In a world so uncaring
With no heart to reveal,
Going by just like me
Viewing her so surreal.
I wish I could stop,
In front of her kneel.
Push her gently back up
So her love could prevail.
With hands of a blessing
Less this minor detail.
If another has noticed
How she might feel,
I guess there is hope
For our planet to heal.

The Queen of Hearts

She can wake you up
Or put you to sleep
She can make you laugh
Or make you weep
She'll teach you to fly
Or stay close to the earth
She'll talk you to death
For all that you're worth
She can lift you high
Choose to lay you low
She'll walk in your shoes
She'll want to know
She asks you read her
Like a paperback book
She is your shadow
She is your hook
She may point at you
But not at herself
She haunts your mind
In sickness or health
She's only a lyric
Of simplest rhyme
If you ask her why
She has no time
But to bid you goodbye
To meet your fate
Then get you dressed
Lest *you* be late.

In The Currency of Deception

Off to the thrift store on a budget analysis,
Trying not to feel I'll get stigmatic paralysis.
I give up tightly fitting in on this cultural chain,
The old credit card trap or a borrower's shame.
I get unforeseen expenses so difficult to arrange,
Tho' I'm older and wiser, the wage hasn't changed.
Deceptive needs or desires, like designer blue jeans,
The softest white tissue on the butt-end of esteem.
Your favorite color a ploy with lace on every edge,
Pure allegiance to fads and fashions we pledge.
Why not barter a friend rather than pile on "stuff"
They have enough clutter: When is enough is enough?
We drown in duplication at the wall-to-wall mart,
I prefer to create a gift straight from the heart.
For a helpful useful gadget vs. another knick-knack,
I'll bend on this principle or take it right back.
This 'process of growth' takes many a bad purchase,
But when you empty your bag it's the only thing worth it.

A Christmas Day Recall

A messenger whispers:

Crystalline
Heaven
Reflects
Inside
Snowbound
Timeless
Memories
Abiding
Solitude.

Drive to go far
Away from a noisy destination
Yearning only for peace.

I am sadly a helpless passenger.

Riding by a glistening white field
Engulfing one small dark silhouette.
Cold air seems to cruelly caress
A lone statuesque horse,
Looking at me
Looking at him.

Petition of Impeachment

Explore the nightmare
Of clouded perception.
Delete the traumas of deception.
I am whole.
I am here,
In this world of Godless prayer.
Where no one else
Can truly hear,
Within the hum of massive fear.
They all look up
To find the steeple
That points the way for wingless people.
God does love.
God does rage,
For leaving blank the final page.
Forever after,
Once upon a time,
The Prosecutor designed the crime.
Stand down mad leader
In global shame.
I cast my torch upon your name.
They can't conceive
I knew you when,
There was a Master to defend.
Disperse us back
To Spirit-space,
Where every woman knew your face.
Hidden eyes,
A fork-split tongue.
You have turned the loaded gun.

Come Together As One

Silence
Inflection
Only the fear
Keeps us here
In this:

Compliance
Disconnection
Only the prayer
Can the Universe hear:

Cadence
Connection
Only madmen dare
Send our children there:

Violence
Indirection
Flag-covered lair
Historically compare
We must beware
We must prepare:

Persistence
Rejection:
Of lies and diversion
These men of perversion
Of the Constitution
One World Institution:

Science
Infection:
Cure with solutions
Expunge the pollution
Of body and mind
War be not kind.

Anatomystics 101

Greet the reader,
Strike a chord.
The Poet Tree,
A two-edge sword.
Nay a riddle
Rhythmic line,
Dance of mystics
Autistics find;
Measure of norms
A circled-in box.
Eyes like windows
Naught interlock.
Emerald Tablets,
The Secret of NIMH,
Binds the Dark,
Defines the Sin.
Born in the grotto
Where oceans speak:
All are One,
Not one unique.
Fear not Death
As it sets you free
From physical chains
Called Humanity.
Sleepy Angels
Around the Flower
It is finally time
Reclaim your Power.
Blood letters and prayer,
Red-inked feather pens,
Shall still the Voices
When we think in Tens.

Tragic Magic

Never wake a sleeping Dragon.
Whisper, lest s/he hear.

Tiptoe in the halls.
Shut windows and doors.
See candlelight and shadows
Flicker and flow.

Listen carefully
Before you walk with me:
He is She.
She is He.
Born of fire.
A fierce Protector,
    shape shifter,
            potential predator.

Curved overgrown claws,
Each a smooth sharp machete,
Resting cold and dormant
On a cement bed
Under a webbed canopy
Dreaming of olde battles.

Taster of metallic salt,
Blood, sweat and tears.
Bittersweet vengeance.
All that's in you.
All that's in me.

Light of Pure Love

O' winged White Angel
Inhale my last breath
Draw me in close
Gently rock me to death
I have lived this hard life
My tale not to be told
Don't scorn me of flight
Not one secret I've sold
I've been banished here
Since I fell to the Earth
Lord return to me wings
Lost at human birth
Empty me of red blood
It has been most defiled
Where I didn't succeed
May I be reconciled
I'll never be worthy
To peer into the Sun
Those who were chosen
Dreamt I to be One
Both relieved and sad
It is soon I must depart
Take away this memory
Rest this broken Heart
Thank you for Guardians
To my front and behind
Return me to pure Love
In the Light unconfined
Please take me back home
I release my Gray Soul
Only merging with You
Shall I be happy and whole.

The Boys of Barronhurst

They say:
No man is an   island.

What about Woman?

This fruit-bearing
Parcel of land.
A haven for all
Who seek comfort
In an Ocean of Tears.

Mother to the Son.

I say:
Each boy taught to pretend
He is indeed an   island,
Raging and resting
In the bosom of the Earth,
Shall always return
To the caul,
Enveloped and
Forever dependent
Upon Her will.

An Outcry Within

Cry out
In sorrow.
Dream high
From low,
Solo

Silhouette.
Celestial grace
Within the rainbow
Aura.

Aurora rising
Upon night fall.
I Am
Afraid to Be
Brave.

Now blindly
I see Ecclesiastes.
Echoes of the past:

Nothing is new
Under this old
Scorching Sun.

Meaningless meaning.
For nothing is real
Except Nothingness.

Majority Rules

What kind of Profession,
Spends years in a Session,
Bickering of inane digression
With no real progression,

Propaganda and Recession
Gives way for Depression
A fear instilled suppression
Of beleaguered oppression

I get the obvious impression
We lost freedom of expression.
In the act of concession
Wanting divine intercession

This now hissing compression
Battling material possession
Like an addictive obsession
Leading to our confession

Only We can stop this regression.
If we join the Civil Procession

As One People,
Under God,
Indivisible.

A Glimpse of Faithe

A Rat unloved
An Angel distant
A rabbit still
The beat persistent
We possess Not
'Cause we fear All
Her broken wing
That empty stall
The dog shall bite
A cat maligned
One mouse escapes
While otters pine
A child's tear
A still born fawn
A blinding glimpse
Of fate gone wrong
I held the squirrel
As she did pass
He who kills
Shall live Life last
When the Lion sighs
A crow not shrill
I'll be standing
On Barren Hill
I'll call the Dove
The Raven low
A serpent cold
From Devil's Row
Listen People!
I'll cry once more
I see you there
Your opaque door
Come first on knee
Sing the Sacred Song
Sing with Unity
Sing clear and strong.

Wondering Saints

Calhoun and Benedict
Thought each a Saint,
While unto God
They shared complaint:
The Word so contradictory
Requires flipping history.

"We walk alone,
The two of us.
A lot of roaches
And choking dust.
No inhabitants
For us to preach,
Best we be deaf
With lack of speech.
We'll wander
With the zero-ones,
For the hell of it
Dig up their guns.
Metal arms of war
And ignoble pride,
Now look at them
They all have died."

Benedict bowed down
Then began to hum,
While Calhoun mumbled
By deaf and dumb.
No people to revere
Their Godly strides,
After the bombing
And Godless lies.

Both walked the desert
And scorned the Sun:
"When does this end
Become begun?"

Plastic and Providence

I'm in exile by the wooden post
No more wings or Holy Ghost
Angels turned their backs on me
Because of frail complicity
You never answered why I was here
What wrong I did when I was there
Why have you groomed a Soul of Grief?
How could you send the Mole and Thief?
I keep returning to this spot
There is no road or open lot
Forest deep and dreary too
Why see why no flowers grew?
Spider web this sticky Fate
What's the point if I escape?
You say submit and unlearn this life
While you hold the sharpest knife
Why reveal the metaphor
And see this failure seven-score?
They cannot listen outside their head
While each is but the walking dead
Yet I'm animate again once more
Plastic as then I was before.

Priest of Leviathan

Dearest Angel of Light
See the reviled thief
Again do discredit
His cunning deceit
He can only read
The Scripture I live
He forswore God's Word
Then mainlined to forgive
His reflective gold wine
Ancient water so cold
His eye on the pyramids
All things bought and sold
He destroys but the Body
I plead release of the Soul
His slaves cry in anguish
While digging his hole

Yea,
Pull up the tripping block
Such is Truth to disturb
Those without voice
Can finally be heard

"Dead Disciple enrobed,
Show us your eyes,
Show us your teeth,
Your patent disguise."

We shall turn our backs
To the threatening winds
Revelation draws nigh
God's rule now begins.

Poem One: Rolling Wild

Shall we become
So uncivilized?
A Hater's Havana?
The Gospel revised?
Our children locked
Under watchful Eye.
The Twenty-Four curfew
The ambivalent cry.
The Supremacist spirit,
With Islamic ferocity,
A Capitol Crime,
A divisive democracy.
Pay off small liberties,
Loan sharks to insure.
Did they call us to war?
If so, then what for?
Such devilization,
A mock demonstration,
A craving for power,
In the fallen nation.

Poem Two: Too Little Be Late

Why seek me now,
Like a last straw
Grasping to sustain
Your failing Law?
You mocked and judged,
You smeared my Name,
Played the nemesis
Of my brain.
You won on one level,
But lost a whole lot.
My voice and poetry
Long left this spot.
Buzzards take you home
You've earned this loss,
Now know that the Master
Is not always the Boss.
I speak no more.
God spare I return.
Crush their pursuits.
Mine Enemy burn.

Poem Three: Rapid Rites

I'm as harmless
As the 'Seuss'
All language
Vague and loose
Not so tight
Nor succinct
Microcosmic
Dark instinct
That must rhyme
To retain
All that clogs
The Great Brain
Oh, fragile muscle
Cooperate with flow
The bloody heart rules
Of things that grow
Or shall you say " No"?
Rebellious pig pride
Only you can create
An opposing fat lie
Truth wins over
The sighing breath
That's all that's heard
In the space of Death.

Poem Four: Matriarch Sing

Steal my rhythm
Match the crime
Old songs die hard
In Modern Time
Lullaby brain
Rock to the beat
This is the armor
They shan't defeat
A nursery rhyme
For the falling reign
Build Her back up
Re-impose Her Name
Balance doth scream:
Return us our Mothers!
Patriarchal Rulers
Hath killed our Brothers
Men in shame withdraw
Beg that She might forgive
Better you heed now
Than to never have lived.

The Eve of Eden

Your world.
You own it.
Cultivate and nurture it.
Weeds to the left,
Watering can to the right.

Sun beams warm,
Scents of spring,
Sweet simplicity
As a small face,
Peering up to You.
Curiously reaching,
Into existence,
Asking the stars:

Am I acceptable,
A mere dandelioness?
Fatefully placed,
In Your garden,
Of mixed soil?

I only offer this moment,
Suspended beauty,
In a reflective pattern.
A nova of brilliance.
Here today,
Tempted.
Gone tomorrow,
Tossed.

An unknowing entry,
Frightening and pure.
A glorious exit,
From eternal captivity.

The Baker Man

The Baker kneaded
A glob of Dough,
Then plopped some pieces
Into a row.
Some got burnt.
Some were chewy.
Some got dry,
Others gooey.
So similar did they appear,
He named them Cookies
To eat and share.
A pattern does actually exist,
Circular squares upon a Dish.
Who can say it has a Date?
A chip or raisin?
Makes for debate.
The criticized nut,
Or clump of flour,
All were created,
To devour.
Some do crumble,
Some do melt.
Who cares what
They might have felt?

Meaningless Meaning

I knew an Elaine
Who tried to explain
The scalding rain
Swept down the drain.

'Twas called mundane,
Yet she'll maintain
Her lasting bane.
Considered insane,
She got profane
And tried to refrain,
In absolute pain
Her utter disdain.

She'd only complain
With nothing to gain.
Nor way to contain
The broken chain
Once used to detain
Or harshly restrain
'Cause others do ordain
The tiniest of grain
From a faulty brain
That cannot abstain
On paper plain
With blue-lined stain
Naught meant to pertain
Lest bother retain
As all is in vain.

So I'm going to read
Ecclesiastes
All over again.

Letting Go of Eisha

(Cancer...
The Haughty Demon;
The Relentless Leech,
The Insatiable, Slithering,
Malignant Beast).

O' my sweet Eisha,
Love in my life,
Cuddling up to me,
A Gentle One,
Peaceful and giving,
Intertwining with my Soul,
My very Breath.
How I loved you.
Letting go ripped,
Flattened me to the core.
Relinquishing your body,
Only added another slash,
To my open wound,
Of Spiritual senselessness.
But I have already experienced,
And faithfully await,
Our Amazing Reunion.

(Cancer...
That malevolent Monster,
Shall crave unto Itself,
Falling into the Abyss.
Powerless,
Unforgotten,
Unforgiven).

Ancestral Ghosts

Less than programmed
Wild our kind
To civil authorities
We've lost our mind
But it is patience
Compassion and game
That set us apart
We have no shame
Your touching lies
Betrayal and religion
Has created our kind
An immortal condition
See you fear Death
We see it as a phase
We regenerate
We don't count days
You are your own enemy
As you reason our reason
We breathe the Creation
While you name the season
Step away! You contagions!
You parasitic Beasts!
We see the jailed freedom
Now your power has ceased
Under all countries
Under all gods
We shall never delay
Nor spare the rod
We control the matter
And what matters most
We are your ancestors
We are your ghosts.

May We All Rise

How can any one say:
Someone is *too* old?
Something is *so* new?
Is it not what it is?
If it's all about you?
Optical illusions,
In comparative frames,
Only mere subjects,
Borrowing names.
Some call this Society,
Others call it The Game.
Bottled perceptions,
Of misfortune and fame.
Acknowledge the signs,
Kind of a song.
See every letter,
The background it's on.
You should not reap,
For souls or gold.
Nor be used,
Not be sold.
Your every mask,
Mirrors The Sinner.
I find he's insatiable,
A sore-losing winner.
You can walk away,
From the looking glass,
No longer run,
See present is past.
Call it what you want,
Opinion is but a wish,
With an opposing view,
This vengeful twist.
All of your concerns,
Interposed with pride,
Disrupts your balance,
And deadens your eyes.

Good To Be Home

A cup of Caffeine,
Medication to cope,
A toke of Nicotine,
A douse of Soap.
I can face anything,
My tank is full.
Drive to the Wasteland,
Avoiding The Bull,
As in a China Shop,
Spending on Crap,
Things I'll only regret,
And can't take back,
Without a snide leer,
Damn, lost receipt!
Give 'em My License,
They sure dig deep!
Databases that sort,
The Best and those Lesser,
Starving Uninsured Numbers,
Laid off Under Pressure.
Kids now Abuse Parents,
Clean out their drawers,
Put them into restraints,
Awaiting such horrors.
But The Plan is intact,
A Pandemic is near,
Obedient Slaves,
Surviving on Fear.
Turning the corner,
Beware of The Fox,
One must feign Invisible,
But for the Metal Box,
Rolling out of The City,
Back to My Zone,
Lock all the doors,
It's good to be Home.

Rainbow Vision 2009

Red and orange
Yellow leaves
Green pine absorb
The autumn breeze
Blue is what
Some people get
Purple wine
Heals all regret
Black is for
The clocks reversed
White is the snow
All life immersed
Opaque is ice
Such frozen pain
Silver is
The tinsel rain
Gold on every
Christmas crown
Silent night
Holy sound
Gray, it hovers
A canopy of gloom
Brown earth is
Renewal soon
So comes the Sun
So warm and bright
It casts no shadow
It is pure Light.

Psalm: 91

Tin soldiers we bought
From China with love
Buddha of the Sword
Pierces the Dove
Tainted dog food
Cars, litter and waste
Poisonous ingestions
Sweet to the taste
Our Eagle flew South
The fallout is coming
There's a Bear in the North
Our delinquents are running
Smoke and dust
Thundering wrath
I don't need my vision
For straight is The Path
Stay in your home
With Ones close at heart
As soon as you see Them
Their televised march
They trample the flowers
The graves of white snow
Mixing blood in the soil
Their numbers just grow
You sold out my country
Now drowning in debt
Rich men shall tremble
Now watch what they get
I have my Bible
Clean Water and Hope
I've got the Name
To help me cope
I've been the human
Witnessing to others
Is this what it takes
To be sisters and brothers?
There's a Man at my door
Drawing a gun
I just continue
Reading Psalm: 91

Of Ants and Men

Worker ant, heed your place
Your purpose is a life of waste
When can you play, dance or sing?
Where is your family for time to bring?
Black, red and brown why must you fight?
Who falsely told you might is right?
You know your farm in an office sits?
It entertains fat hypocrites
Little ant do retreat
Step aside to hear defeat
And when it comes to fall asleep
Be the soldier, not herded sheep
Kings and Queens, Jacks of the knife
Think nothing of your tiny life
Pack the children tucked in bed
Whisper the Truth inside their head
The Master's shoes sit paralyzed
Until he's awake to recognize
No more Workers want his Lie
Here the plate reads "Live Free or Die".
Tell the world to pull his plug
He is nothing but a Mega-Thug.

Time After Time

To ride the crooked line end or fore
Who invented that revolving door?
This is yesterday, the future is here
Can you hear me now from far or near?
Stop the watch and tend to your present
Do you know when it's real or fluorescent?
Does light pain your eyes scanning skies?
Is it worth two-cents you save to drive?
Every gallon claims your destination
Blood does fuel this revelation.
I'm wringing out a rag of Truth
You're as old as your remembered youth
Shall we simplify the paperwork?
Start to step outside or go beserk
Take it to dump it or it clutters your brain
Recycle their thoughts or they shall drain
Your actual life you should be living
The Puppeteers are so misgiving
Who is your Master that owns your Soul?
Burn a dollar bill in his brass-rimmed bowl
He'll cast a frown like a blackened cloud
Don't deliver the rainbow to his shroud
War is his cry and vengeance his aim
Protect your children from the flame
Of greed, deception and conformation
Now do you know the correlation?
I speak only from historical mention
Well, this is just another dimension
Same story from the Book of Lies
He who imitates surely dies.

What If Then?

When it snows
There shall be ice
Where there are men
There will be strife
When you birth words
Then tell everyone
They are your captives
Until you're done
If you watch TV
Then you are there
You replay the scene
Though unaware
You spend the money
That isn't yours
What you really need
Is not in stores
You mark the years
With celebration
Or idle time
In hibernation
Who owns the land
Where you build your road?
Are you reaping seeds
That you have sowed?
When comes dark rain
It may never end
I know you've wondered
What if and then?
The sun returns
So you forget
You remain predictable
What did I expect?

Detachment

We medicate
To levitate
Above this hell
Beyond the spell
Am I decrepit
If I stand alone
An original sin
Fully grown?
So imperfect
I'm immobilized
Can't begin
To fraternize
As I recall
My mother's past
I feel condemned
And failing fast
I drug this body
Into submission
Can't kill the cancer
With sharp precision
I read The Word
Then peer outside
I am speechless
And so I hide
This is shame
To pay the price
A thousand times
A thousand mice
I admire the rodent
Who minds his way
A simpler survival
To sleep all day
The night is solace
For the human soul
Sedation sought
So I've been told
Anesthetize me
In the end
I'm too tired
To start again
In this I'll surrender
Not lead nor gloat
My head is heavy
And yet I float.

Psalm 2011

Time reversed
When all was mud
After Noah
And the flood
The angels landed
Lizards crawled
All of paradise
Had dissolved
Powers collided
In war and strife
The Hunter prowled
Seeking Life
The Tree of Knowledge
Stood petrified
Lightning struck
From every side
The land erupted
The waters stilled
This was the start
Of what was willed
A challenge was made
God turned away
That was then
As it is today
The earth is scarred
Wildlife has perished
Not even Love
Is truly cherished
They did choose
What mattered most
Themselves of course
For this thcy boast
God please return
We remember not
How now it's twice
Ours seeds do rot
Too many paths
Have been made
Reveal the Truth
For this we've prayed
Trap the wicked
Cast the snare
Deliver your children
Everywhere.

Origin of a Pulse

The rudder of a boat
The tail of a plane
Feather of a bird
Medulla of the brain
So need these parts
To ride the tide
Soar the air
Or hide inside
The power resides
In a very small thing
People think it's large
Or hidden in a ring
There's an auric flight
Beyond life and death
Without this awareness
You'll gasp for breath
The illusion is physical
A material high
There's another location
Not seen by the eye
"I" am an obstacle
When I walk and react
When I think of my feet
I feel the impact
Yet I am really you
As you make me whole
Because the Spirit is a Flame
Dancing over the Soul
Propelling us forward
Through time and space
Merging our existence
In rhythmic grace.

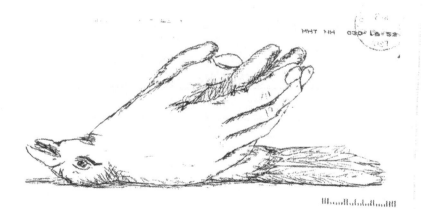

CELLMARK
NO. 25065
NHSP

Artwork by: Edward Keith,
A talented and very special brother.
c. 1997 Cellmark

About The Author
About The Book

The author identifies much with C.S. Lewis and ironically, Dr. Seuss. A rhythmic rhyme and a somewhat serious pose molds well in the mind of most readers. It's likened to a sound bite from any effective commercial we seem to instinctively think or utter in response to other events. Words are very elastic in that they can at once be stretched out into parts and twisted into some karmic circle while maintaining their original posture.

Just as we try to understand some of our experiences, Ms. Louise has done the same by poetically magnifying into verse the questions that arise in many familiar situations. Human behavior is scrutinized as an oxymoron. Her "MagArt", is another way to alter messages that are always approved of in manipulative advertising.

Her work began at the age of fourteen and has been chronologically documented by date keeping up with current events both personally and globally. This autobiographical collection was compiled into a self-published book covering the years of 1977-2003 entitled: *A Part of Me For that Part of You*.

Now comes the following eight years during which swift changes have occurred for Ms. Louise personally and politically. This new title, ***Poetically Correct: Banned by The Free Press***, was assumed, due to an encounter with a newspaper, after many years of publishing her work with them, in which they claimed that 'freedom of the press' had **only** to do with... the freedom of the press to pick and choose what they will and will not print. This author felt perplexed because her words are not of slander or threat. Her poem, *"Sunday Hypocrite"* was the first to be rejected as not fit for the public in "their" opinion.